Performing the State

Performance measurement is now a key management tool used by government to assess and enhance public services. It is also used as a tool for public sector transparency and accountability. Despite these noble objectives, performance measurement can also generate counter-productive and sometimes paradoxical outcomes. This book innovatively conceptualises performance measurement as a 'policy instrument'. Such an approach necessarily invites careful and critical examination of instances of the formation, application and contestation of particular performance measurement regimes, the tools used to measure performance, the way in which performance data is produced and used, and the complex dynamics between professionals, managers and service users that arise from these practices. The book provides detailed empirical examples of performance measurement in the delivery of health, schooling and child welfare services, as well as the problematics of assessing national wellbeing. Instead of a form of scientific and rational management, performance measurement is revealed as an intrinsically contested, socio-politically charged and value laden practice. The book concludes that to succeed in delivering authentic performance improvements public sector managers must be aware of these complex, paradoxical dynamics and the circumstances that make performance measurement perform.

This book was originally published as a special issue of *Policy Studies*.

Paul Henman is Associate Professor of Digital Sociology and Social Policy at the University of Queensland, Australia. His research examines the nexus between government policy, public administration, and information technologies. He is the author of *Governing Electronically: E-government and the reconfiguration of policy, public administration and power* (2010).

Alison Gable is an Honorary Research Fellow in the Schools of Education and Social Science at the University of Queensland, Australia. Her research and practice sits at the intersection of data, professions, education policy, and reform.

Performing the State
Critical Encounters with Performance Measurement in Social and Public Policy

Edited by
Paul Henman and Alison Gable

LONDON AND NEW YORK

First published 2018 by Routledge

2 Park Square, Milton Park, Abingdon, Oxfordshire OX14 4RN

52 Vanderbilt Avenue, New York, NY 10017

Routledge is an imprint of the Taylor & Francis Group, an informa business

First issued in paperback 2019

Copyright © 2018 Taylor & Francis

All rights reserved. No part of this book may be reprinted or reproduced or utilised in any form or by any electronic, mechanical, or other means, now known or hereafter invented, including photocopying and recording, or in any information storage or retrieval system, without permission in writing from the publishers.

Notice:

Product or corporate names may be trademarks or registered trademarks, and are used only for identification and explanation without intent to infringe.

British Library Cataloguing in Publication Data

A catalogue record for this book is available from the British Library

ISBN 13: 978-1-138-10458-7 (hbk)
ISBN 13: 978-0-367-89109-1 (pbk)

Typeset in Minion Pro
by RefineCatch Limited, Bungay, Suffolk

Publisher's Note

The publisher accepts responsibility for any inconsistencies that may have arisen during the conversion of this book from journal articles to book chapters, namely the possible inclusion of journal terminology.

Disclaimer

Every effort has been made to contact copyright holders for their permission to reprint material in this book. The publishers would be grateful to hear from any copyright holder who is not here acknowledged and will undertake to rectify any errors or omissions in future editions of this book.

Contents

Citation Information — vii
Notes on Contributors — ix

Introduction – Performing the state: the socio-political dimensions of performance measurement in policy and public services — 1
Paul Henman

1. Performance measurement as a policy instrument — 10
Patrick Le Galès

2. Population health performance as primary healthcare governance in Australia: professionals and the politics of performance — 23
Michele Foster, Paul Henman, Alison Gable and Michelle Denton

3. Hitting the target without missing the point: New Zealand's immunisation health target for two year olds — 37
Esther Willing

4. The challenge of quantifying national well-being: lessons from the *Measures of Australia's Progress* initiative — 53
Cosmo Howard and Amber Chambers

5. NAPLAN data: a new policy assemblage and mode of governance in Australian schooling — 70
Alison Gable and Bob Lingard

6. Repositioning prevention in child protection using performance indicators — 85
Clare Tilbury

7. Techniques and paradoxes in performing performance measurements: concluding reflections — 99
Paul Henman

Index — 113

Citation Information

The chapters in this book were originally published in *Policy Studies*, volume 37, issue 6 (November 2016). When citing this material, please use the original page numbering for each article, as follows:

Introduction
Performing the state: the socio-political dimensions of performance measurement in policy and public services
Paul Henman
Policy Studies, volume 37, issue 6 (November 2016), pp. 499–507

Chapter 1
Performance measurement as a policy instrument
Patrick Le Galès
Policy Studies, volume 37, issue 6 (November 2016), pp. 508–520

Chapter 2
Population health performance as primary healthcare governance in Australia: professionals and the politics of performance
Michele Foster, Paul Henman, Alison Gable and Michelle Denton
Policy Studies, volume 37, issue 6 (November 2016), pp. 521–534

Chapter 3
Hitting the target without missing the point: New Zealand's immunisation health target for two year olds
Esther Willing
Policy Studies, volume 37, issue 6 (November 2016), pp. 535–550

Chapter 4
The challenge of quantifying national well-being: lessons from the Measures of Australia's Progress *initiative*
Cosmo Howard and Amber Chambers
Policy Studies, volume 37, issue 6 (November 2016), pp. 551–567

Chapter 5
NAPLAN data: a new policy assemblage and mode of governance in Australian schooling
Alison Gable and Bob Lingard
Policy Studies, volume 37, issue 6 (November 2016), pp. 568–582

CITATION INFORMATION

Chapter 6
Repositioning prevention in child protection using performance indicators
Clare Tilbury
Policy Studies, volume 37, issue 6 (November 2016), pp. 583–596

Chapter 7
Techniques and paradoxes in performing performance measurements: concluding reflections
Paul Henman
Policy Studies, volume 37, issue 6 (November 2016), pp. 597–609

For any permission-related enquiries please visit:
http://www.tandfonline.com/page/help/permissions

Notes on Contributors

Amber Chambers is affiliated with the Department of Sociology, Gender and Social Work at the University of Otago, New Zealand.

Michelle Denton is a Research Fellow in the School of Nursing, Midwifery and Social Work at the University of Queensland, Australia.

Michele Foster is Professor of Disability and Rehabilitation Research, School of Human Services and Social Work, Menzies Health Institute Queensland at Griffith University, Australia.

Alison Gable is an Honorary Research Fellow in the Schools of Education and Social Science at the University of Queensland, Australia.

Paul Henman is Associate Professor of Digital Sociology and Social Policy at the University of Queensland, Australia.

Cosmo Howard is a Senior Lecturer in the School of Government and International Relations, and member of the Centre for Governance and Public Policy, Griffith University, Australia.

Patrick Le Galès, FBA, is CNRS Research Professor in Politics and Sociology at the Centre d'Etudes Européennes, and Dean of the Urban School, Sciences Po, France.

Bob Lingard is a Professorial Research Fellow in the School of Education and the Institute of Social Science Research at the University of Queensland, Australia.

Clare Tilbury is the Leneen Forde Chair of Child and Family Research at the School of Human Services and Social Work at Griffith University, Australia.

Esther Willing is a Lecturer with Te Kupenga Hauora Māori at the University of Auckland, New Zealand.

Performing the state: the socio-political dimensions of performance measurement in policy and public services

Paul Henman

ABSTRACT
This opening paper outlines the rise of public sector performance measurement and performance governance from New Public Management, its trajectory from an administrative tool for organisational monitoring and management, to its insertion into service performance and accountability, to a policy tool defining policy itself. Four key conceptual ways of approaching public sector performance measurement are outlined, and the significance of understanding performance measurement as a socio-technical policy instrument is argued. The paper thematically reviews the papers that follow and how they demonstrate new points of critical analysis in policy studies, including the multiple, mixed and sometimes contradictory purposes for performance measurement, the formation of performance measurement tools, the linkages of performance numbers and governance structures from macro to micro, and the reconfigured roles of professionals in public service delivery. The paper issues a clear challenge to policy researchers to take performance measurement more seriously in understanding the dynamics of policy performance, the achievement of policy objectives, the reframing of policy and the experience of citizens.

Introduction

Performance measurement is now indisputably embedded into the core functioning of the state. Its presence and impact is evidenced in the design, administration and evaluation of public policy, the operation of state and non-state organisations, the conduct of government workers and contractors, and the delivery of government funded services. Indeed, performance measurement is but a component of many tools, practices and people that constitute a larger 'performance regime' (Talbot 2008). This constellation includes performance indicators, data and targets, key performance indicators (KPIs), performance reports, governance practices, legislation and so on. The ubiquity of performance technologies within contemporary government in the developed world suggests the arrival of a 'Performance State'. Thus, the Performance State is not only evidenced by the widespread use of performance measurement, defined as the enumeration of organisational or system-level processes, outputs and outcomes (cf Dooren, Bouckaert, and Halligan 2015, 20), but as a constellation of problematisations and grammar of 'performance' – performance indicators, targets, KPIs, benchmarking, quality assurance and performance governance – that are capillaries of rationalised power entangled within all processes of government.

Performance measurement in the public sector has received considerable attention in the academic disciplines of public administration and management where the focus is largely on the 'technical' aspects of performance measurement, such as designing good measuring instruments and organisational practices, creating effective performance governance arrangements, and the impact performance measurement has on organisational and public sector performance (Lewis 2015). Embedded in this literature is the notion that performance measurement and its concomitant realities are a technical matter of public governance; that within the classical (and contested) divide between 'elected politicians that make public policy in the political realm' and 'professional public servants that judiciously and compliantly administer the policy in a politically neutral fashion', the academic study of performance measurement is primarily located in the latter.

Yet, performance measurement increasingly has important public policy implications and requires critical attention. If 'what is measured is what counts', performance measurement can be seen to displace established substantive and wide-ranging public policies and practices to focus on achieving measurement scores. This dynamic is evident in the debate about benchmark testing in schools creating a narrowing of the curriculum (Polesel, Rice, and Dulfer 2014), and about whether maximising GDP is the best way to ensure national well-being (AGPN 2009). In such debates, the critique is that the performance measurement becomes the default policy, displacing the substantive one.

Further, performance measurement has at times become the substantive public policy, specifically when setting performance targets as the policy objective. For example, when governments agree to cut carbon emissions by a given percentage by 2020 (UNFCC 2008), or when former British Prime Minister accounted he would half child poverty by 2010–2011 (Blair 1999), or when then Australian Prime Minister Julia Gillard announced that Australian schools would rise to the top five countries in the Programme for International Student Assessment (PISA) (Gillard 2012), then public policy *is* achieving a performance target. In doing so, public policy is irretrievably connected to specific performance measurements and the particular way they enumerate the world.

One does not even need to mention the presence of gaming and fraud in performance measurement processes (Bevan and Hood 2006; de Bruijn 2007) to see that the objectives, mechanisms and achievements of public policy can be substantially recast by performance measurement. Accordingly, public and social policy scholars need to take a much greater interest in performance measurement for what it means for the conduct of the state and the lived effect of policy.

Indeed, there is increasing evidence of critical analysis of performance measurement in a wide range of public services and policies (see Lewis 2015; Trommel et al. 2004). Such analysis operates within specific policy domains – such as schooling (Gable and Lingard), public or primary health (Foster et al, Willing), well-being (Howard and Chambers) and child protection (Tilbury) – as is done in this special edition. This is an important beginning point. What is needed is a wider consideration of performance measurement, the comparative similarities and disjunctures that cross jurisdictions and policy/service domains, and its constitution of the Performance State. Towards this longer-term goal, Le Galès in this edition proffers the notion of policy instruments (see also Lascoumes and Le Galès 2007) as one possible conceptual framework for systematically analysing different manifestations of performance measurement.[1]

In establishing the groundwork for this special edition, this paper first outlines the rise of performance measurement in the public sector. It then reviews different approaches for conceptualising performance measurement, before providing an overview of the papers that follow.

The making of the Performance State

It is uncontroversial to argue that the proliferation of public sector performance measurement in OECD countries is a function of the installation of New Public Management (NPM) rationalities and practices from the 1980s onwards (Christensen and Lægreid 2002; Lane 2000; Osborne and Gaebler 1993). Although there is debate about what constitutes the NPM organisational approach, a constellation of business and market-inspired management designs and practices are regularly referred to in defining it. Pollitt, for example, lists eight key elements of NPM:

(1) shifting the focus of management systems from inputs and processes towards outputs and outcomes;
(2) shifting towards measurement and quantification, especially through the development of performance indicators and performance targets;
(3) a preference for more specialised, 'lean', 'flat' and autonomous organisational structures, sometimes expressed as allowing managers the freedom to manage (managerialism);
(4) a substitution of formal, hierarchical relationships between or within organisations by contracts or contract-like relationships (contractualism);
(5) greater use of market models or market-type mechanisms for the delivery of public services (marketisation);
(6) emphasising service quality and consumer/customer focus;
(7) broadening and blurring the boundaries between the public sector, the market sector and the non-profit sector (mixed economy) and
(8) shifting value priorities away from universalism, equity, security and resilience towards efficiency and individualism (2003, 27–28).

The presence of performance measurement in this account of NPM is unmissable in points one and two. Less evident is the key role in performance measurement in other dimensions of NPM. For example, the centre is capable of governing by numbers aggregated and disaggregated at the centre to make visible the various parts of an organisation or network, thereby displacing governance by detailed top-down rules. Consequently, reporting performance data, rather than rules, becomes the *sine qua non* of managerialism, contractualism, marketisation and the consequent mixed economy (points 3, 4, 5 and 7 above). So too does point six become enacted by performance measurements with customer service KPIs and benchmarking (Clarke et al. 2007). Alongside the dynamic of moving measurement from inputs, to outputs and outcomes (point 1), there has also been a clear extension of public performance measurement of operational matters (such as finance and human resources matters) to policy objectives, from the readily numerable (such as money, people, numbers of service events) to the less so (such as satisfaction, quality and learning), and from public bureaucrats to professionals. There has been a dynamism of numeration and commensuration to make the capillaries of the state visible.[2]

It would, however, be a mistake to assume that performance measurement is essentially neo-liberal in character. Indeed, as Goa (2009) makes clear in the case of China, performance measurement has been a critical characteristic of public management in command and control countries. Rather, performance measurement is better viewed as a technology within a rationalist scientific approach to management that has a history in early twentieth-century Fordist time and motion studies, cost accounting (Miller 1990; Miller and O'Leary 1987) and beyond.

A second mistake is to interpret the installation of performance measurement into public governance only in terms of organisational efficiencies and effectiveness or neo-liberal dreams of marketised, minimal states. Performance measurement and reporting is also closely connected to the 'audit society' (Power 1997) and associated rationalities of public accountability and transparency. These too are connected with democratic ideals of making the public sector accountable to citizens and 'tax payers'. Citizen rights' activism and consumer-rights also provide the normative basis for performance measurement, as does the increasingly marketised delivery of public services whereby performance measurements afford consumer-citizens (Clarke et al. 2007) with a means to facilitate choice (Graham 2014).

Such diverse political discourses provide the necessary intellectual basis for the proliferation of performance measurement. They demonstrate that socio-political dimensions of performance measurement go well beyond the political agenda of NPM. The capacity of performance measurement to be a key feature offering a solution to this variety of political imperatives is impressive, and highlights its tool-like status. Nevertheless, the discourses do not provide the required material mechanisms for their operation. It is not coincidental then that the growing hyper-dynamic of performance measurement occurs alongside increasingly networked digital information and communication infrastructures that intensify the collection, storage, circulation and calculation on digital data (Henman 2010). Such technologies provide new ways in which to know the State and intervene in its operation, actors and service users. This is certainly worthy of critical appraisal.

Conceptual approaches to public sector performance measurement

There are at least four broadly different approaches to conceptualising and analysing public sector performance measurement and its dynamics, each arising from different academic disciplines and different analytical objectives.

A first approach to conceptualising public sector performance is to locate it within the principal-agent 'problem'. In this perspective, agents undertake tasks on behalf of the principal. However, information asymmetry arises, especially in specialised and complex tasks, and makes it difficult for the principal to externally monitor the agent (Talbot 2008, 1569). By measuring the activity or outcome of the agent's conduct, performance measurement provides the means with which to assess the agent's performance. From a rational choice perspective, making visible an agent's performance makes the agent more accountable and incentivises the agent to perform, which can be further managed by imposing rewards or punishments. In this framework, measurement has effects. Firstly, it makes performance visible, and then governable (Miller 2001). While providing powerful insights, this conceptualisation of performance measurement provides a flat description of human behaviour and elides the much more complex dynamic environment in which most performance measurement takes place.

A second approach, evident in much public administration and management literature, is to locate performance measurement within a broader public performance problem, of how to evaluate and enhance public sector performance. This approach characterises public sector performance like a machine with inputs, processes, outputs and outcomes; a production model of performance. This traditional diagram of performance locates performance measurement as a technical tool with which to evaluate performance, as evidenced by outputs or outcomes; and in relation to organisational or policy objectives (Bouckaert and Halligan 2007; Dooren, Bouckaert, and Halligan 2015, Figure 2.1) and wider contexts (Pollitt and Bouckaert 2011; Talbot 2010). In this framework, performance measurement is assumed to be an inert object that objectively and independently measures the operations and effects of public sector operations. The analytical concern is of validity and reliability, to work out how best to measure performance and how to attribute inputs and processes to measured outcomes. Consequently, the socio-political dimensions and effects of performance measurement remain invisible in this framework. Moreover, the framework posits unproblematically the notion that a public sector agency (or state) has a 'performance' and it can be quantified.

A third approach abstracts beyond this second one to characterise and compare different systems of public performance governance (Bouckaert and Halligan 2007). Embedding the framework of the second approach outlined above, this approach focuses on the governance frameworks within which public sector performance is measured and how performance information is reflexively fed back into agency or sector deliberations and governance processes (see also Moynihan 2009). These conceptual developments are helpful in conceptualising and locating performance measurement as a rationalised governance tool within public sector processes, however such frameworks are poor in providing analytical focus on the tool itself, its socio-political construction, use and effects. In short the above focus on the problematic of performance (albeit problematically), not the problematic of performance measurement. For the latter, an alternative approach is required.

A fourth way to conceptualise performance measurement is as a policy instrument or tool. This approach directs analysis of the location, use and effects of the tool. The recent work of Lascoumes and Le Galès (2007; Le Galès 2011) emphasises such socio-technical and political character of policy instruments, not simply as technical responses to governance, but also socio-political ones. Conceptualising performance measurement as a policy instrument is our starting point, as outlined below.

Overview of this special edition

This special edition of *Policy Studies* has been curated in order to provide insights into performance indicators from varied public policy and service domains (namely, education, health, child and family services, and national well-being). While the papers are empirically based primarily in Australasia, they are located within similar public policy and service developments, discourses and challenges in many OECD countries.

By presenting detailed empirical studies of performance measurement in different geographical, organisational, service and policy locales, new insights about the socio-political dimensions and dynamics of performance measurement can arise. Spaces and occasions of similarities and differences can be observed and evaluated. Overall, the papers are located with the perspective of performance measurement as a policy instrument, as articulated by Le Galès and Lascoumes. That framework is concisely presented and considered especially in relation to performance measurement in the paper by Patrick Le Galès. While the empirical papers presented in this edition make various use of this policy instrument approach, it is by reading the papers from this perspective that the strength of this edition and its wider contribution becomes clearer.

In concert with material ontologies and philosophies (Latour 2005; Verbeek 2010), Le Galès' paper makes the case that policy instruments, of which performance measurement is but one example, must be understood not a simple neutral devices, but objects that have their own effects. This means that policy instruments deserve critical examination themselves, of their social lives and histories (cf Law, Ruppert, and Savage 2011) and make-up. In viewing performance measurement, and policy instruments more broadly, their materiality and affordances, it becomes possible to more critically analyse their role in governing, and their proliferation over the last few decades. Within Lascoumes and Le Galès' categorisation of policy instruments, performance measurement can act as both an incentive-based instrument and an information/communication-based instrument. As Le Galès notes, these are constitutive of different political relations, respectively, the mobilising state and audience democracy.

This duality of performance measurement is also evident across the papers in this edition. In the case of both school educational performance (Gable and Lingard) and primary health care governance (Foster et al.; Willing), the rationale for performance measurement is presented as both an incentive-based instrument and an information/communication-based instrument, the latter particularly pertinent with the public publication of comparative performance/league tables and discourses of consumer choice. Yet, this duality is also a space for contestation, politicisation and confusion about the 'real' purposes of performance measurement.

Such contestation reinforces the validity of the policy instrument approach to include a critical focus on the measurement tool itself. While typical management analyses focus on the 'technical' aspects of a performance indicator such as issues of construct validity and administrative feasibility, the policy instrument approach extends its gaze to the socio-political dimensions of these considerations. Howard and Chambers' paper on Australia's attempts at constructing national well-being indicators that go beyond the well-recognised limitations of GDP nicely captures this mix of technical and socio-political analyses. On the one hand, measuring national well-being faces considerable construct validity issues due to the nebulous nature of the concept of collective well-being. On the other hand, the concept of collective well-being is also deeply contested as it can embed different socio-political, philosophical and ontological versions of what constitutes well-being. Howard and Chambers' paper also highlights how the technical design of a multi-measurement approach to national well-being has failed in both political and policy discourse because it does not have the technical authority that a single measure presents with its objective like stature. The socio-political contestation of the 'right' measure is a key focus of Tilbury's paper that challenges the policy appropriateness of recommended

KPIs in recent child protection reforms. Interestingly, the only paper in which the performance measurement itself is not contested is Willing's examination of immunisation rates in New Zealand.

Another important dimension across many of the papers involves the micro–macro linkages of performance measurement. The ability to aggregate and disaggregate performance numbers from nation, to systems/regions (e.g. States, educational/health districts), to organisations (e.g. schools, universities, general practices (GP)), to individuals (e.g. teachers, students, doctors) is a key affordance arising from the technical design of a performance measurement. This numerical linkage from micro to macro is evident in Willing's account of immunisation measures and Gable and Lingard's account of educational performance, but the capacity to do so is a politically charged and organisationally and technically difficult endeavour in Foster et al.'s study of improving population health outcomes through primary health care providers.

Alongside these numerical linkages operates formal governance arrangements that either facilitate the upwards and downwards coupling of performance measurement with performance management (Power 2014) or disrupts (aspirations for) these flows. A common theme is the creation of new performance organisations and actors to enable the downwards propulsion of performance governance. Willing notes the creation of immunisation champions and collaborative inter-organisational immunisation networks, while Gable and Lingard observe Assistant Regional Directors – School Performance as new key roles with which to focus performance governance. On the other hand, Foster et al. examine the contested and seemingly intractable problem of creating regional primary health care organisations in Australia located between the Federal government and private, market-based GPs in order to govern and generate community health outcomes.

A further dimension arising from the papers is the reconstitution of professionals, their practices, rationalities, and their enduring attachment to professional discretionary judgement. Tilbury notes how proposed KPIs in child protection impose a normative black/white evaluation on professional practices in out of home care ('bad') and family services ('good'), which systemically displaces professional judgement about what is in the 'best interests of the child' and in turn can generate highly negative outcomes for some children and parents. In contrast to much push-back by professionals who see performance measurement as a reduction of professional autonomy (as evidenced by Foster et al.), the papers by Willing and Gable and Lingard demonstrate how professionals can incorporate performance measurement into professional self-reflection and self-governance, as an additional element within or reconfigured conception of professional autonomy (see also Henman and Gable 2015).

In concluding, this special edition practically demonstrates several intellectual contributions. First, conceptualising performance measurement as a policy instrument widens the critical analytical space in which to understand, engage with and contest the socio-political dimensions of performance measurement in public policy and services. As such it reinforces the acute need for policy studies to examine performance measurement, and not to leave it to management and organisational studies, as performance measurement not just measures performance, but subtly and substantially reconfigures the nature of policy and services, thereby affecting policy actors, service providers, professionals and citizens. Finally, the collection illustrates the analytical benefits of comparing performance measurement in different policy, jurisdictional and organisational locales in order to tease out the dynamics that bring real benefits and those that do more damage to collectively shared policy objectives (see concluding paper in this issue).

Notes

1. See also Henman et al. (2014) for a more comprehensive analytical framework to support critical social analysis of performance measurement.
2. This dynamic parallels the rapid enumeration of the state through the census and statistics from the eighteenth century onwards (Desrosières and Naish 2002; Higgs 2004).

Disclosure statement

No potential conflict of interest was reported by the author.

Funding

This paper arose out of research funded by an Australian Research Council Discovery Project grant [DP110100803].

References

AGPN. 2009. *Connecting Care*. Canberra: Australian General Practice Network.
Bevan, Gwyn, and Christopher Hood. 2006. "What's Measured is what Matters." *Public Administration* 84 (3): 517–538.
Blair, T. 1999. "Beveridge Lecture." Speech at Toynbee Hall, London, March 18.
Bouckaert, Geert, and John Halligan. 2007. *Managing Performance*. London: Routledge.
de Bruijn, Hans. 2007. *Managing Performance in the Public Sector*. London: Routledge.
Christensen, Tom, and Per Lægreid. 2002. *New Public Management*. Aldershot: Ashgate.
Clarke, John, Janet Newman, Nick Smith, Elizabeth Vidler, and Louise Westmarland. 2007. *Creating Citizen Consumers*. London: Sage Publications.
Desrosières, Alain, and Camille Naish. 2002. *The Politics of Large Numbers*. Cambridge, MA: Harvard University Press.
Dooren, Wouter van, Geert Bouckaert, and John Halligan. 2015. *Performance Management in the Public Sector*. New York: Routledge.
Gillard, J. 2012. "A National Plan for School Improvement." Speech to the National Press Club, September 3.
Goa, Jie. 2009. "Governing by Goals and Numbers." *Public Administration and Development* 29 (1): 21–31.

Graham, Tim. 2014. "Technologies of Choice." In *Challenging Identities, Institutions and Communities: Refereed Proceedings of the TASA 2014*, edited by Brad West, 1–13. Adelaide: TASA.

Henman, Paul. 2010. *Governing Electronically*. New York: Palgrave Macmillan.

Henman, Paul, and Alison Gable. 2015. "'Schooling' Performance Measurement." *Policy & Society* 34 (1): 63–74.

Henman, Paul, Elizabeth Strakosch, Alison Gable, Michele Foster, Bob Lingard, Richard James, and Mitchell Dean. 2014. "Multidimensional Analysis of Performance Measurement Systems (MAPS) in public governance." Working paper, University of Queensland.

Higgs, Edward. 2004. *The Information State in England*. New York: Palgrave Macmillan.

Lane, Jan-Erik. 2000. *New Public Management*. New York: Routledge.

Lascoumes, Pierre, and Patrick Le Galès. 2007. "Introduction: Understanding Public Policy through its Instruments." *Governance: An International Journal of Policy, Administration, and Institutions* 20 (1): 1–21.

Latour, Bruno. 2005. *Reassembling the Social*. New York: Oxford University Press.

Law, John, Evelyn Ruppert, and Mike Savage. 2011. *The Double Social Life of Methods*. Manchester: Centre for Research on Socio-Cultural Change.

Le Galès, Patrick. 2011. "Policy Instruments and Governance." In *The SAGE Handbook of Governance*, edited by Mark Bevir, 142–160. London: SAGE.

Lewis, Jenny. 2015. "The Politics and Consequences of Performance Measurement." *Policy & Society* 34 (1): 1–12.

Miller, Peter. 1990. "On the Interrelations between Accounting and the State." *Accounting, Organizations and Society* 15 (4): 315–338.

Miller, Peter. 2001. "Governing by Numbers." *Social Pratices* 68 (2): 379–396.

Miller, Peter, and Ted O'Leary. 1987. "Accounting and the Construction of the Governable Person." *Accounting, Organizations and Society* 12 (3): 235–265.

Moynihan, Donald P. 2009. "Through a Glass, Darkly." *Public Performance & Management Review* 32 (4): 592–603.

Osborne, David, and Ted Gaebler. 1993. *Reinventing Government*. New York: Plume Book.

Polesel, John, Suzanne Rice, and Nicole Dulfer. 2014. "The Impact of High-stakes Testing on Curriculum and Pedagogy." *Journal of Education Policy* 29 (5): 640–657.

Pollitt, Christopher. 2003. *The Essential Public Manager*. Philadelphia, PA: Open University Press.

Pollitt, Christopher, and Geert Bouckaert. 2011. *Public Management Reform*. Oxford: Oxford University Press.

Power, Michael. 1997. *The Audit Society*. Oxford: Oxford University Press.

Power, Michael. 2014. "Organizations and Audit Trails." Working Paper, London School of Economics.

Talbot, C. 2008. "Performance Regimes." *Public Administration* 31 (14): 1569–1591.

Talbot, C. 2010. *Theories of Performance*. Oxford: Oxford University Press.

Trommel, Willem, Taco Brandsen, Mirjan van Heffen-Oude Vrielink, and Maaike Moulijn. 2004. "Performance Measurement in Public Governance." *Society and Economy* 26 (2/3): 195–221.

UNFCC. 2008. *Kyoto Protocol Reference Manual on Accounting of Emissions and Assigned Amount*. Bonn: United Nations Framework Convention on Climate Change.

Verbeek, Peter Paul. 2010. *What Things Do*. University Park: The Pennsylvania State University Press.

Performance measurement as a policy instrument

Patrick Le Galès

ABSTRACT
The rise of government by indicators, by figures may reveal a new wave of rationalization organized by the state in the classic Weberian sense. Contemporary forms of government are marked by the rise of indicators, measures and new metrics to compare, certify, codify and evaluate. In many countries, performance measurement has become one of the symbols of the transformation of governance. The paper aims to show how performance indicators are a particular type of policy instrument that increases competitive pressure within societies even if that cannot be analysed only in terms of neoliberalism.

The instruments of the performative state

As the great political scientist Christopher Hood puts it in the phrase 'Welcome to the ranking world', and in the delights of what Paul Henman analyses as the 'Performance State' in the introduction, measuring, quantifying, evaluating have become massive activities in the contemporary world. Once again, Max Weber was correct; those activities reflect relations of domination alike in the private and the public sector.

The rise of government by indicators, by figures may reveal a new wave of rationalization organized by the state in the classic Weberian sense. Many papers in the special issue bear witness of this trend. On the other hand, the state is not only performative, it is also performed. In other words, the state (together with large firms) is a massive quantifier and producer of measures and ranking. But the state is part of a globalizing world. The state is also increasingly being quantified, measured (Fourcade 2016; Lemoine 2016). In the neo-Marxist or neoliberal account, the contemporary state (the Schumpeterian globalizing workfare state as once suggested by Jessop (2002)) is mobilizing society for generalized economic competition. One account of neoliberalism is the idea of the disciplining of the state by private sectors measures, metrics and indicators, rating agencies with the use of financial indicators. The performative state might be the result of those transformations.

There are many ways to think about the transformation of states, from the interdependance with capitalism, to the rise of neoliberalism, the transformation of violence and war, the rationalization of state organizations, the impact of democratic pressure, the role of migration (King and Le Galès 2016). Contemporary forms of government are marked by the rise of indicators, measures and new metrics to compare, certify, codify and evaluate. In many countries, performance measurement has become one of the symbols of the transformation of governance. Various groups of scholars inspired by Foucault, Weber, Bourdieu, the sociology of science and technology, the sociology of quantification and management studies have documented the rise of measurement, and quantification, for instance Michael Power with his classic book *The Audit Society* (1999).

Several schools of thought have developed to make sense of this transformation and importance of measurement of performance and quantification. Historically, the development of statistics, measures and categories was associated with the development of the modern state (Porter 1995; Didier 2009). Even more incisively, sociologist and statistician Alain Desrosières has developed critical thinking about the making of the metrics of the state to rationalize, 'Seeing like a state' (Scott 1998). In his classic book on *The Politics of Large Numbers* (2010), Desrosières makes a compelling case showing the relationship between the rise of statistics, of various measurements and the increasing role of the state over time. In Europe in particular, the state was the master of measure, of categories. In order to make the society legible (Scott 1998), the modernist state used all sorts of census, measures and calculations in order to prepare the war, to mobilize populations, to tax, in other words, to govern its territory and population as Foucault eloquently put it. Foucault's insight was precisely to decentre the analysis of the state in order to show different modes of *étatisation* of society; that is, the use of new technologies and dispositifs. In Britain, the group of critical scholars within business schools that started the journal *Accounting, Organization and Society* produced a wealth of incisive analysis and criticism of performative instruments. Nowadays, US cultural and economic sociology is developing a whole range of understanding processes associated with forms of measurement, valuation and evaluation (Fourcade 2011; Lamont 2012). The making of different metrics also produces and reveals different forms of inequalities (Espeland and Stevens 1998; Lawn and Normand 2014)

The paper aims to show how performance indicators are a particular type of policy instrument that increases competitive pressure within societies even if that cannot be analysed only in terms of neoliberalism. It starts by showing how the policy instrument approach has been elaborated in relation to Weber and Foucault. It then shows how policy instruments such as indicators of performance are central to the restructuring of states.

Policy instruments and technologies of government

Together with Pierre Lascoumes, and later with Charlotte Halpern, I have suggested that the rise of policy indicators should be analysed in terms of policy instruments, They are a concrete modality of exercising power revealing the structures of domination in the Weberian sense. Over the past decade, reflection on policy instruments and on public policy instrumentation in particular has shaped debate and fuelled in-depth discussions in relation to the rise of managerialism, forms of neoliberalism and the production of data associated with new technologies (Hood and Margetts 2007).

The contributions in our book *Gouverner par les instruments*, published in 2004 and the 2007 special issue of the journal *Governance*, sought to contribute to the policy debate. At the time, public policy – which falls within political sociology – was dominated by approaches that centred on stakeholders, ideas and institutions. We thus shifted our focus to the technologies of government. Social scientists studying the state and government have long taken an interest in the issue of technologies of government, including its instruments – Weber and Foucault, for instance.[1]

Michel Foucault took up this subject in his own way and pointed out the importance of what he called the 'technical procedures' of power – that is, 'instrumentation' – as a central activity in 'the art of governing' (Sennellart 1995). In a 1994 text, he formulated his programme for the study of governmentality as an approach that

> does not revolve around the general principle of the law or the myth of power, but concerns itself with the complex and multiple practices of a 'governmentality' that presupposes, on the one hand, rational forms, technical procedures, instrumentations through which to operate, and, on the other, strategic games that subject the power relations they are supposed to guarantee to instability and reversal. (Foucault 1994)

Foucault contributed to the renewal of thinking on the state and governmental practices by shunning conventional debates of political philosophy about the nature and legitimacy of governments, devoting himself instead to their materiality, their policies and their modes of acting. In his reflections on the political, he put forward the question of the 'statization of society' – that is, the development of concrete devices, instruments, practices functioning more through discipline than constraint, and framing actions and representations of all social actors. He then refers to the contribution of the cameral sciences, to show the basis of his approach.

It was in the late 1960s that Foucault, in the context of his work on political liberalism, turned his attention to the writings of the cameral sciences (Foucault 1998). This science of police – that is, of the concrete organization of society – took shape in Prussia in the second half of the eighteenth century; it combined a political vision based on the philosophy of *Aufklärung* (Enlightenment) with principles that claimed rationality in administering the affairs of the city (Sennellart 1995). This current in rationalist thought was gradually displaced by 'populationist concern for the happiness of populations', combining dimensions of public order, well-being and culture. In classical political philosophy (e.g. Jean Bodin's sixteenth-century work), there was an important separation between the attributes of sovereignty and the administration of everyday life. In contrast, from the late seventeenth century, there was a search for unity in the exercise of power, and these two dimensions came to be gradually integrated. Thus, the cameral sciences were the melting-pot of contemporary public policies. In his argument, Foucault distinguishes three stages in the development of this type of knowledge (1998) an initial stage of critical utopia, where the conceptualization of an alternative model of government enabled implicit criticism of the monarchical regime. He refers to Louis Turquet de Mayenne, who, in 1611, envisaged the development of a specialization of executive power – 'police' – to look after both the productivity of society and the security of its inhabitants. He saw this as a fourth 'major function', alongside the classic attributes of the royal prerogative: the judiciary, the army and the exchequer.

A second stage took shape at the beginning of the eighteenth century, when the general movement towards rationalization was applied to the royal administration by some of its officials, who were concerned for better efficiency. Various treatises made proposals for bringing order to the forest of royal regulations, and devoted themselves to the tasks of listing, classifying and categorizing in order to foster the organization of public policy. One of the most famous in Europe was written by Nicolas Delamare, who published his *Traité de la police* in 1705. According to him, 'happiness (that is, "individual security and prosperity") is a requirement for the development of the state', and it is the responsibility of the political to achieve this objective.

Finally, a third stage was marked by the creation, mainly in Germany, of *Polizeiwissenschaft*, a more theoretical approach, which also became an academic discipline. Foucault's reference work here is Johann Von Justi's *Elements of Police* (1756), which proposed principles for action in 'taking care of individuals living in society' and aimed to 'consolidate the citizen's life with a view to fostering the state's strength'. Training academies were developed. These welcomed the future civil servants of Prussia, Austria and Russia, who were to promote various administrative reforms in their countries. This current of thought spread more widely throughout Europe, and is viewed as having inspired some Napoleonic reforms of the executive.

This view, focused on the cameral sciences, led Foucault to clarify his thinking on analysis of the political. First of all, he pointed out the importance of differentiating between *Politik* and *Polizei*. This distinction is important, since *Polizei* has its own dual political rationality. One rationality is that of aim – the aim of expressing the interdependence between the productivity of civil society and the state's strength. This is complemented by a rationality of means, viewing religious faith and love of sovereign or republic as insufficient for the construction of the collective. This second rationality must be filtered through concrete practices relating to security, the economy and culture (education, health, trade, the arts, etc.), which are just as much essential tasks of the state. For him, the central issue was not the democratic or authoritarian nature of the state; nor did it relate to the essence of the state or to its ideology, factors which legitimize or fail to legitimize it. He looked from the opposite end of the telescope, taking the view that the central issue was that of the statization of society – that is, the development of a set of concrete devices, practices through which power is exercised materially. Foucault proposed to analyse 'practical systems' (1998). That is, not to consider societies as they present themselves or to question the conditions that determine these representations, but rather to apply himself to what they do and the way they do it. This led him to propose a study of the forms of rationality that organize powers. Finally, in analysing practices, he stressed that the exercise of discipline was at least as important as constraint. Contrary to the traditional concept of an authoritarian power functioning through handing down injunction and sanction, he proposed a disciplinary concept that was based on concrete techniques for framing individuals, allowing their behaviours to be led from a distance.

The legacy of this thought has been remobilized, in the contemporary period, to account for changes in modes of government/governance. Focusing on policy instruments is a way to link sociological analysis of forms of rationalization of power to the public policy tradition that is looking at new linkages between public authorities and economic and social actors in an internationalized context, for means of regulation and for the reshaping of the state. It is therefore argued that the study of policy instruments and processes of instrumentation is crucial to any investigation of the reshaping of the state or of public policy change.

Instrumentation of public policy and reshaping of the state

The dynamics of growth of the state during the twentieth century were accompanied by the development and diversification of public policy instruments and by the accumulation of programmes and policies in the different sectors where the state intervenes. Perhaps more surprisingly, processes of reshaping the contemporary state have been accompanied by a new wave of innovations relating to these instruments, notably but not exclusively in recently expanded areas of public policy, such as policies on risk (environmental risks, health risks, etc.), the regulation (statutory or otherwise) of the market, building infrastructures, running utilities, and state or welfare state reforms.

In addition to the question of who governs – as well as who guides, who directs society, who organizes the debate about collective aims – there is now the question of how to govern increasingly differentiated societies. States are parties to multinational regional logics of institutionalization (for instance the EU), to diverse and contradictory globalization processes, to the escape of some social groups and to economic flows, to the formation of transnational actors partly beyond the boundaries and injunctions of governments. Within the EU, for instance, the state no longer mints coins, no longer makes war on its neighbour; it has accepted the free movement of goods and people, and a supranational central bank. Enterprises, social mobilizations and diverse actors all have differing capacities for access to public goods or political resources beyond the state – the capacities for organization and resistance that, in the 1970s, brought out the theme of the ungovernability of complex societies (Mayntz 1993). This literature has reintroduced the issue of instruments, through questions about the management and governance of public subsystems of societies and policy networks.

The proliferation of actors and coordination instruments in an ever-increasing number of sectors has brought out a new paradigm: 'the new governance' or 'new negotiated governance' (Salamon 2002), in which public policies are less hierarchized, less organized within a sector demarcated or structured by powerful interest groups (e.g. urban policy, environmental policy, new social policies or the negotiation of major infrastructures) – at the risk of denying the interplay of social interests and of masking power relations. Over and above deconstructing this issue (as well as the limits of government and failures of reform), research into government and public policies has highlighted the renewal of public policy instruments either for the development of depoliticized formulas in 'the new governance' or through fostering powerful mechanisms for the control and direction of behaviours (Hood 1998).

On the basis of the British case, even constant modification of instruments can be seen as significant, in that this obliges the actors to adapt all the time, 'running along behind' instruments that are constantly changing in the name of efficiency and rationality (Bevan and Hood 2006). This instrumentalization of the instrumentation considerably increases the degree of control by central élites and marginalizes the issue of aims and objectives even further – or at the very least, euphemizes them. From this angle, public policy instruments may be seen as revealing the behaviours of actors, with the actors becoming more visible and more predictable through the workings of instruments (an essential factor from the point of view of the state's élites) (Power 1999).

We deliberately focused our research programme on the practical aspects and material elements of these activities and on representations. Put differently, we focused on instruments, tools and devices as originally highlighted by management sciences and by the sociology of science and technology. These studies led to a comprehensive review of the intermediaries of collective action which were enhanced and occasionally accorded an agent status that was partly autonomous and oriented stakeholders' behaviour (Akrich, Callon, and Latour 2006). This approach has gradually spread to different fields within the social sciences. Beyond the sociology of science and technology, the approach is today used to analyse markets, capitalism, business and different forms of collective action linked to government.

We used the instrument approach to more fully grasp public policy as empirically, our attention had been drawn to the significance of instruments and of public policy instrumentation in many sectors (urban, environment, Europe, finance, etc.). Instruments are not only highly effective in tracing change (jostling history, revealing discrete scenes), they are also among the variables that explain the dynamics observed such as the production of new expertise or the renewal of coalitions (Lascoumes and Le Galès 2007).

We thus distanced ourselves from three widespread assumptions: the technical neutrality of instruments; their indifference to political strategies and fascination with instrumental innovation. Our perception of instruments as specific types of institutions was based on the premise that instruments make it possible to focus on changes in the relationship between the governing and the governed, as well as on the various forms of managing complex societies.

The proliferation and overlapping of instruments were particularly discernible in a number of sectors in recently expanded areas of public policy such as health and environmental risks, market regulation or state reform fields (Halpern 2010). Nevertheless, many other fields in which state intervention had been a longstanding practice in specific sectors such as education, housing and transport were also marked by similar developments and the rise of indicators in particular. Based on this first phase, *Gouverner par les instruments* enabled us to define the concepts of 'instrument' and 'instrumentation'. It also made it possible to develop a typology of the forms of political relationships structured by instruments, in line with different forms of legitimacy (Table 1), and to propose empirical tests.

For us a *policy instrument* is a device that is both technical and social. It structures specific social relations between public authorities and those it is addressed to, according to the representations and meanings it conveys. *Instrumentation* refers to the set of problems posed by the choice and use of instruments (techniques, methods of operation, devices) that allow government policy to be made material and operational.

Table 1. A summary of the typology of policy instruments.

Type of instrument	Type of political relations	Type of legitimacy
Legislative and regulatory	Social guardian state	Imposition of a General Interest by mandated elected Representatives
Economic and Fiscal	Wealth producer state and redistributive state	Seeks benefit to the community, social and economic efficiency
Agreement-based and incentive-base	Mobilizing state	Seeks direct involvement
Information-based and communication-based	Audience democracy	Explanation of decisions and accountability of actors
Performance indicators standards best practices	Adjustments within civil society, competitive mechanisms	Mixed: Scientific/Technical, democratically negotiated and/or competition, pressure of market mechanisms

Source: Lascoumes and Le Galès (2004, 351).

A number of researchers have since used the instrumentation framework to enhance policy analysis (Halpern, Lascoumes, and Le Galès 2014). The emphasis placed on instruments has contributed to discussions on policy change and innovation, on the emergence and resolution of conflicts, and on the phenomena of inertia, resistance and restructuring. These studies have confirmed the relevance of debate on the strengths and weaknesses of the 'policy through instruments' approach to explain phenomena observed empirically. Our initial perspective of instruments proves deeply perceptive due to the transformation of political regulation and the restructuring of the state, and has also made it possible to associate them with studies on the exercise of power. By using this approach in a systematic and comparative manner to explore the relationship between instrumentation and the modes of government and governance in Europe, we have tested the solidity and limitations of this category of analysis. We have also reflected on the modalities of its operationalization and demonstrated how and within what contexts using particular types of instruments can be beneficial or not.

Performance indicators have massively increased over the last two decades, as several papers of this special issue are showing. Based upon our emphasis of political regulation, the use of indicators of performance may be seen as an alternative to classic instruments such as taxes or legislation or agreements, charters and other instruments of negotiated governance. The generalization of performance indicators may reveal a difficulty to exercise authority. States have less capacity to exercise authority by relying upon classic coercion. Instead of using law, taxes or mobilization, states might be looking for new forms of legitimacy that is always fragile. Performance indicators are easy to put forward as evidence of states on the move, objectively improving whatever objectives are identified. They also reflect a more hands off policy to governance rather than a direct intervention to impose sanctions, or an expensive policy. This type of instruments may in other words be read as the rise of a more regulatory state. The political dimension as much as the technical dimension are essential.

Those performance instruments allow the imposition of objectives and competition mechanisms and exercise strong coercion. They are used in particular when the government does not trust the actors, and may pretend to avoid direct negotiation. The search for effectiveness or efficiency relies upon incentives and a metrics of performance that is supposed to guide the action of actors. They have to adapt, to face those competitive pressure … or be sanctioned. That relates to an understanding of state as performance enhancer, aiming towards the strengthening of competitiveness, but also a state that is classically creating the categories of action, stabilizing representations of problems, indicating priorities. As Espeland and Sauder (2007) emphasized, processes of commensuration lead to rankings, new hierarchies. Those hierarchies and indicators of performance may be national or increasingly beyond the nation state. As mentioned, in economic terms, in matter of education, health or environment, states are more and more ranked and performed by transnational organizations.

With my colleague Scott (2010), I have argued that the use of policy performance indicators should be analysed as a 'new bureaucratic revolution',[2] to use the words of Max Weber, transforming the forms of the exercise of power in both private and public organizations. We tried to show how the strength of institutional change and how the public sector imitates the private, that is, how the state initiates and implements a parallel approach to the one pioneered in the private sector in steering and governance. In other words, in line with Weber, we argued that on the one hand, state policies precede the extension of the market and development of capitalism and, on the other, that the state then imports or imitates the way large-scale enterprise is organized into its own practices. Instead of accepting the understanding that state and market are opposed, it seems worthwhile to us to reconsider the notion that they are interdependent, a classic sociology theme for conceiving of how the social order is formed and how actors' behaviour is rendered predictable.

Performance measurement as a form of state rationalization

There are of course many ways to conceptualize the state (Leibfried et al. 2015). Ongoing conceptual debates about the nature of the state and what constitutes statehood are both intimidating and fascinating. Among other things, as a working classic definition, the state might be seen as a set of institutional apparatuses, bureaucracies and organizations developed to increase the capacity of the state to control and govern a given territory to penetrate and organize social life.

The state itself is increasingly differentiated. It seems to be a series of enmeshed agencies, organizations, flexible rules and negotiations with an increasing number of actors. Public policy is characterized by ad hoc or contingency arrangements and enmeshed networks, by the random, by a proliferation of actors, multiple aims, heterogeneity, cross-linking of issues and changes in the scales of reference geographies. The capacity for direction of the state is subject to challenge; it seems to be losing its monopoly, is less the centre of political processes or of conflict regulation hence the importance of measurement to rationalize.

The contemporary question of measurement and quantification is part of the agenda of state restructuring. In Western Europe and in the US, empirical research points to different, sometimes contradictory directions about transformations of the state. A large body of research has also tried to identify state failures. The contemporary debate about the state, very much influenced both by comparative political economy research and by the governance question, tends to focus on the question of capacity (King and Le Galès 2016). State activities, from measurement to policies, have become an essential feature of state restructuring.

In the late 1990s, Crouch and Streeck (1997) joined an increasing number of scholars who pointed towards decreasing capacity of the state to govern society. The argument is well known: globalization trends, however contradictory they might be, may give a role to the state to force the adaptation of society but they also make society more difficult to govern because of the rise of exit strategies of firms and economic flux in particular. The hidden secret of the state was therefore one of a growing inability to govern society, to tax, to implement decisions. This scholarship developed a new research agenda based upon classic questions associated with governance and government alike: not just who governs but how governments and various actors involved in governance processes operate. This is not a new idea. Foucault in particular made the point about the importance of shifting patterns of governmentality and the theme was central for Rose and Miller when they started their long-term research programme on the same phenomenon (2007).

Political economy scholars, emphasizing the role of the globalization of capitalism, have even more developed the idea of the powerless state in economic terms or at the very least of the state heavily constrained by financial markets, the strategy of large firms or globalized exchanges. In a recent contribution to this debate, Mertens and Streeck (2013) have precisely underlined the fiscal crisis of the state.

By contrast many scholars also pointed out, at the same time that state operations, public policies were expanding in new spheres (Levy 2006). States have become more intrusive or have developed new policies in not only matters of education, gender, discrimination, environment, but also security, defense and surveillance. New bureaucracies are developing in the field of auditing and control to change the behaviour of individuals through mechanisms of sanctions and rewards. In terms of relations between states and markets, neo-Marxist, Polanyian and neoinstitutionalists have for long stressed the fact that markets were sustained by state activities, policies, ideologies and finances. As Levy rightly documents (2006), the rise of market making activities and policies has become a notable feature of state elites more influenced by neoliberal ideas. In Britain for example, both the Thatcher and the New Labour governments were characterized not only by privatization and the introduction of market mechanisms in the public sector, but also centralization, and a stronger and more authoritarian state (Gamble 1994; Faucher-King and Le Galès 2010). In the US, a whole series of research emphasized the same apparently contradictory patterns (Jacobs and King 2009).

All this is often put forward as the triumph of new public management or of the neoliberal bureaucratization of the state or demonstrating the hegemony of some neoliberal governmentality.[3] This is part of the story, but one may suggest a different argument: the reconfiguration of the state is explained by the need to overcome policy failure, to rationalize, to find new ways to 'penetrate', to orientate society (Mann 1984), to discipline, to recover capacity to govern, to change behaviour. New ways have evolved to impose coercion, to rationalize, to discipline society that give rise to the regulatory state.

From the Sociology of Science to Social History, from Economics to Management, taking instruments and instrumentation into account often prompts reflection on broader issues such as the functioning of markets, the rationalization of action, the shifts in capitalism, the renewal of the modes of domination, the triumph of neoliberalism and/or of new public management and depoliticized policy routines.

Quantification and/or neoliberal governmentality?

Focusing on instruments and on public policy instrumentation from the outset has enabled us to engage in dialogue with the sociology of numbers, indicators, quantification and standardization. These studies on numbers and statistics, benchmarking and rankings comprehend instruments as technologies of government that associate knowledge and power. Clearly, measurement and quantification are not neutral. They result from conflicts and struggles that revolve around definition. They produce outcomes and create new social spaces or institutions. The calculation methods associated with these technologies of government create new inequality metrics (Desrosières 2014). In the introduction of his recent book (2014), Desrosières brought to the fore this new momentum:

There have emerged new instruments and new procedures that can be described as the politics of numbers for some or the politics of large numbers for others (that is, involving the law of large numbers and its convergence properties). On one hand is quantification, within the meaning of transforming words into numbers: accounting results, performance indicators, policy evaluation and ranking, and benchmarking. On the other are probabilistic econometric models, evidence based policy, and profiling of 'individuals at risk' selected through the observed frequency of microsimulation procedures that lead to changes among populations based on stochastic models.

This momentum can be interpreted in terms of the long-term process of rationalization. Nevertheless, by interpreting Foucault from a constructivist perspective (and leaving aside all constraints), a large number of researchers pursuing governmentality studies have focused on the analysis of new forms of domination by attempting to highlight the forms of neoliberal governmentality using devices and instruments (Rose and Miller 2007). Do all these instruments define neoliberal governmentality? This is what British studies, predominantly marked by the Thatcherite revolution, have sought to study. In their book, Dardot and Laval (2013) characterize the new globalized neoliberal ideology as a combination of the ground rules applying to contemporary capitalism and the state's exercise of power. They argue that this ideology continuously steers individuals' behaviour for the benefit of the market society. All the instruments previously mentioned by Desrosières can thus be considered as the tendency of contemporary states to strengthen the market society, by a strong mobilization of the instruments that structure competition, performance and sanctions.

Evaluations and audits can both be decisive neoliberal policy instruments whose aim is the formation of market societies. Nevertheless, our analysis is somewhat different. The neoliberalization of the state – at least over the last 30 years – has undoubtedly been a general trend in the changes observed in many countries, France included. This has resulted in the adoption of a few specific instruments that have focused on measurement in particular. However, let us break away – at least for the moment – from the relative determinism of these authors.

First, a large part of the quantification or the strengthening of the spirit of managerialism does not fall under neoliberal dynamics. The logic of the rationalization of activities, including through measurement and quantification, has a long history. Historically, the 'scientific' approach to government based upon indicators has been central in the communist regime. Economists in the USSR had developed sophisticated techniques for the plans. Similarly in the aftermath of the success of Keynes, statistical techniques were developed to plan and organize economic activities. Observable changes in the instrumentation and logic of rationalization are sometimes linked to the development of new technologies such as computers or communication. Contemporary policy studies have shown that policy often fails, and that the impasses in public regulation have been behind the introduction of new instruments. Instrumentation in terms of cooperation (contracts) is at least as important as instrumentation in terms of norms, standards or indicators that seek to re-orient collective or individual actions. Finally, the dynamics of quantification and classification are also at work, independently from the state, and at its margins arguably driven by different rationalities. A number of social movements have developed practices and instruments and participated in evaluation. Consumers and service users in the health and environment sector in particular, aided by social networks, have prompted the development of ranking to lift the veil of ignorance, confront authority, challenge the opacity of professional practices, hold the authorities accountable and maybe build trust (Jeacle and Carter 2011).

Quantifying approaches go well beyond neoliberalism and it can be difficult to distinguish between the different logics at work. The emergence of managerial practices classified under the term 'new public management' can also be explained by the strategies of bureaucratic elites struggling to regain their capacity to inspire action (Bezes 2007). Reinforcing bureaucracy and rationalization is not necessarily linked to neoliberalism; this does not exclude one specific type of neoliberal instrumentation. Does this neoliberal rationality govern the world? Many forces push in this direction but resistance is equally strong. Describing all these transformations as 'neoliberal bureaucratization' as many authors suggest therefore seems to be a generalization that obscures diverse processes. The papers in this special edition rather support this argument.

Conclusion

Policy instruments such as performance indicators are most of the time likely to have an impact, but how they are used and the resistance they meet can change everything and transform them. Focusing on instrumentation makes it possible to avoid the functionalist reification of instruments (the resolution of problems) and the limitations of constructivism (actors do not invent everything, all the time, and their trajectory often explains nothing of significance). Empirically, instrumentation involves associating reflection on the development and choice of instruments with their implementation in order to identify their uses and understand their outcomes. There are products and instrumentation outputs in terms of the choice and selection of specific procedures of policy implementation through instruments, budgets, rules, norms and standards. But one may also identify outcomes observed over the medium or long term in terms of the (in) ability of policies to organize a policy field and influence social behaviour through conflict resolution, the allocation of resources and the imposition of sanctions. In some cases, instrumentation thus acts as an intermediary variable, a structuring mechanism in the relationship between instruments and the structuring of public policy.

The more societies become complex, the more the rationality associated with measurement may be stressed and made visible. It may reveal collective process to define and implement policy goals or a new wave of illusion of rationality in order to feed the neoliberal beast and discipline society. The dynamics may reinforce some hierarchies between them.

Notes

1. These paragraphs owes much to my colleague Pierre Lascoumes:
2. Weber used the term 'bureaucratic revolution' to characterize the ways in which individual conduct is changed 'from without' by altering the conditions to which they must adapt. In his analysis, bureaucracy as a revolutionary force stands opposed to the other great revolutionary force, charisma.
3. Neoliberalism is a serious issue. But Dean (2014) eloquently makes the point about the overblown use of neoliberalism.

Acknowledgements

Thanks to Paul Henman for comments and the invitation to the workshop organized at the University of Queensland in Brisbane.

Disclosure statement

No potential conflict of interest was reported by the author.

References

Akrich, M., M. Callon, and B. Latour. 2006. *Sociologie de la Traduction*. Paris: Presses de l'Ecole des Mines.
Bevan, G., and C. Hood. 2006. "What's Measured Is What Matters: Targets and Gaming in the English Public Health Care System." *Public Administration* 84 (3): 517–538.
Bezes, P. 2007. "The 'Steering State' Model: The Emergence of a New Organizational Form in the French Public Administration." *Sociologie du Travail in English* 49 (Suppl.): e67–e89.
Crouch, C., and W. Streeck, eds. 1997. *Political Economy of Modern Capitalism*. London: Sage.
Dardot, P., and C. Laval. 2013. *The New Way of the World, on Neoliberal Society*. London: Verso.
Dean, M. 2014. "Rethinking Neoliberalism." *Journal of Sociology* 50 (2): 150–163.
Desrosières, A. 2010. *The Politics of Large Numbers*. Cambridge: Cambridge University Press.
Desrosières, A. 2014. *Prouver et Gouverner*. Paris: La Découverte.
Didier, E. 2009. *En Quoi Consiste l'Amérique? Les Statistiques, le New Deal et la Démocratie*. Paris: La Découverte.
Espeland, W. N., and M. Sauder. 2007. "Rankings and Reactivity, How Public Measures Recreate Social Worlds." *American Journal of Sociology* 113: 1–40.
Espeland, W. N., and M. Stevens. 1998. "Commensuration as Social Process." *Annual Review of Sociology* 24: 313–343.
Faucher-King, F., and P. Le Galès. 2010. *The New Labour Experiment*. Stanford, CA: Stanford University Press.
Foucault, M. 1994. "La Gouvernementalité." In *Dits et écrits, III*, edited by Michel Foucault, 635–657. Paris: Gallimard.
Foucault, M. 1998. "La Technologie Politique des Individus." In *Dits et Ecrits, IV*, edited by Michel Foucault, 813–828. Paris: Gallimard.
Fourcade, M. 2011. "Cents and Sensibility: Economic Values and the Nature of 'Nature' in France and America." *American Journal of Sociology* 116 (6): 1721–1777.
Fourcade, M. 2016. "State Metrology: The Rating of Sovereigns and the Judgment of Nations." In *The Many Hands of the State*, edited by Kimberly Morgan and Ann Orloff. Cambridge University Press.
Gamble, A. 1994. *The Free Economy and the Strong State*. Basingstoke: Palgrave.
Halpern, C. 2010. "Governing Despite its Instruments? Instrumentation in EU Environmental Policy." *West European Politics* 33 (1): 39–57.

Halpern, C., P. Lascoumes, and P. Le Galès, eds. 2014. *Instrumentation de l'action Publique*. Paris: Presses de Sciences Po. (forthcoming in English, Oxford University Press).
Hood, C. 1998. *The Art of the State*. Oxford: Oxford University Press.
Hood, C., and H. Margetts. 2007. *The Tools of Government in the Digital Age*. Hampshire: Palgrave Macmillan.
Jacob, L., and D. King, eds. 2009. *The Unsustainable American State*. New York: Oxford University Press.
Jeacle, I., and C. Carter. 2011. "In Trip Advisor We Trust: Rankings, Calculative Regime and Abstract Systems." *Accounting, Organization and Society* 36: 293–309.
Jessop, B. 2002. *The Future of the Capitalist State*. Cambridge: Polity.
King, D., and P. Le Galès. 2016. *Reconfiguring European States in Crisis*. Oxford: Oxford University Press.
Lamont, M. 2012. "Toward a Comparative Sociology of Valuation and Evaluation." *Annual Review of Sociology* 38: 201–221.
Lascoumes, P., and P. Le Galès. 2007. "Understanding Public Policy Through its Instruments." Special issue. *Governance* 20: 1–21.
Lascoumes, P., and P. Le Galès. 2004. *Gouverner par les Instruments*. Paris: Presses de Sciences Po.
Lawn, N., and R. Normand. 2014. *Shaping of European Education. Interdisciplinary Approaches*. London: Routledge.
Le Galès, P., and A. Scott. 2010. "A British Bureaucratic Revolution? Autonomy Without Control or 'Freer Actors More Rules'." *English Annual Selection, Revue Française de Sociologie* 51 (1): 119–146.
Leibfried, S., E. Huber, M. Lange, J. Levy, F. Nullmeier, J. D. Stephens. eds. 2015. *The Oxford Handbook of the Transformation of the State*. Oxford: Oxford University Press.
Lemoine, B. 2016. "Measuring and Restructuring the State: Debt Metrics and the Control of Present and Future Political Order." In *Reconfiguring European States in Crisis*, edited by D. King and P. Le Galès. Oxford: Oxford University Press.
Levy, J., eds. 2006. *The State after Statism*. Cambridge: Harvard University Press.
Mann, M. 1984. "The Autonomous Power of the State: Its Origins, Mechanisms and Results." *Archives Européennes de Sociologie* 25: 185–213.
Mayntz, R. 1993. "Governing Failure and the Problem of Governability." In *Modern Governance*, edited by J. Kooiman, 9–20. London: Sage.
Mertens, D., and W. Streeck. 2013. "Public Finance and the Decline of State Capacity in Democratic Capitalism." In *Politics in the Age of Austerity*, edited by Armin Schäfer and Wolfgang Streeck, 26–58. Cambridge: Polity Press.
Porter, T. 1995. *Trust in Numbers: The Pursuit of Objectivity in Science and Public Life*. Princeton, NJ: Princeton University Press.
Power, M. 1999. *The Audit Society: Rituals of Verification*. Oxford: Oxford University Press.
Rose, N., and P. Miller. 2007. *Governing the Present*. Cambridge: Polity Press.
Salamon, L. 2002. *The Tools of Government, A Guide to the New Governance*. New York: Oxford University Press.
Scott, J. 1998. *Seeing like a State*. New Haven: Yale University Press.
Sennellart, M. 1995. *Les Arts de Gouverner*. Paris: Le Seuil.

Population health performance as primary healthcare governance in Australia: professionals and the politics of performance

Michele Foster, Paul Henman, Alison Gable and Michelle Denton

ABSTRACT
A range of institutional and financial instruments has been used to drive population health outcomes in primary health care in Australia. However, GP sovereignty and the corporatized nature of general practice have generated major challenges. The core of government reform strategy since 1992 has been the creation and financing of Primary HealthCare Organizations (PHCOs), in various forms, to provide an organizational basis to connect GPs to population health performance, and a closer link between the state and GPs. The shift from Divisions of General Practice, the first PHCO, to Medicare Locals (MLs) in 2011 was notable. The latter constructed the object of performance as a raft of broader population health goals, which were framed in terms of accountability to communities through public reporting. Drawing on interviews with Federal government, health professional associations, ML executives and GPs, this paper examines the ways in which such performance instruments were imagined and understood, and areas of contestation. The findings show the different rationalities at play and how different actors seek control of the policy space. They also demonstrate the political precariousness of PHCOs, and the wider difficulty of steering market-based professionals in the achievement of population health objectives.

Introduction

A high-performing primary healthcare sector is the answer for many western welfare states seeking cost-effective population health outcomes amidst rising healthcare costs, a growing chronic disease burden and consumer and community expectations. Primary health care in Australia comprises medical services, allied health services and a range of other primary health and community services. This component of primary health care is largely market-based; funded by government via Australia's universal health insurance scheme (Medicare), private health insurance and patients. The cornerstone of the sector is general medical practice. General medical practitioners (GPs) play an important gate-keeper role, sitting at the interface between primary health care and complex, high-cost healthcare services and the wider community (Britt et al. 2014; Duckett and Willcox 2011). General practice is now characterized by large 'corporately owned and professionally managed entities that provide some of the support once provided by national organizations, thus lessening ties to those organizations' (Coote 2009, 60). Due to the multiple goals of state involvement and financing in this sector (e.g. curative medicine, population health, access and equity), the governance structure for this sector has attracted increasing government interest. Yet, integrating this sector with the broader healthcare system to improve population health outcomes has proved challenging (Dunbar 2011; Scott and Coote 2010).

The core of government reform strategy has been the creation and financing of Primary HealthCare Organizations (PHCOs), in various forms, to provide a closer link between the state and essentially a fee-for-service, 'individualistic general practice cottage industry', increasingly reliant on public funding, though disconnected from the broader healthcare system (Pegram, Sprogis, and Buckpitt 1995, 79). Divisions of General Practice were the first iteration of the PHCO playing a major part in institutionalizing performance standards but also protecting self-regulation as the mode of accountability (Scott and Coote 2007). Importantly, this government-funded organizational mechanism was expected to strengthen the role of GPs in population-based health and data collection (O'Connor and Peterson 2002; Rogers and Veale 2000a). In 2011, Divisions of General Practice were replaced with an alternate form of PHCO, known as Medicare Locals (MLs), and in 2015 these became Primary Health Networks (PHNs). This new organizational entity sought to address the apparent failure of 'traditional command and control approach to monitoring cost, activity and output data' (Gardner, Sibthorpe, and Lonstaff 2008, 8) and incentive-based policy instruments (Le Galès 2011) to achieve population health objectives. In essence, this new meta-instrument was designed to enable traditional governance mechanisms to work more effectively (Kassim and Le Galès 2010).

Sitting between the Federal government and primary healthcare professionals, the new ML PHCO had responsibility to monitor, manage and publicly report on population health performance using a raft of national standards and performance measurements. Moreover, as a local governance network, covering specified geographical areas, the PHCOs were expected to engage a diversity of clinicians, services and healthcare recipients in generating improved population health outcomes for communities. With a shift away from the GP-centric mode of governance this represented a new organizational field and an altered concept of population health (McDonald et al. 2013). However, as the divisional structure showed, the PHCO mode of governance faced the power of professionals in controlling the implementation space (Rogers and Veale 2000a, 2000b). While Divisions improved organizational performance around population health by way of improved information collection and electronic communication (Scott and Coote 2010), GPs generally resisted control of the clinical domain where they practiced professional accountability to individual patients (Marjoribanks and Lewis 2003). Similarly, population health performance objectives of the new PHCOs could be displaced or disrupted by professionals with clinical autonomy who operate within a market-based setting. We argue that the new PHCOs could generate potential discord because of the different rationales of performance held by the various stakeholders. The premise of our argument is that GPs are likely to adopt a view of performance that is traditionally linked to professional values, norms and self-governance. Performance for the GP therefore will be based around the effectiveness of clinical interactions to improve their patients' outcomes. In contrast, the new PHCOs will adopt a concept of performance based on geographically defined population health outcomes and accountability to a broader community. In that respect, the PHCOs will seek to reposition GPs and general practices within a broader managerial framework of accountability, beyond individual patient encounters and individual practices. To that end, population health performance is likely to be a contested terrain for the various stakeholders and potentially resisted by professionals. The effectiveness of PHCO population health governance is therefore contingent on understanding performance rationalities and the challenges for professionals in delivering performance.

In this paper we draw on the analysis of interviews with GPs and PHCO and policy stakeholders during early implementation of the ML to examine the various performance logics and tensions. First, as a backdrop to the research, a brief review of the key reforms involving PHCOs and implications for governance of population health outcomes is provided. This discussion draws on the concept of policy instruments as modes of governance (Kassim and Le Galès 2010; Lascoumes and Le Galès 2007; Le Galès 2011).

The role of divisional PHCOs in performance governance in Australia

The establishment of the Divisions of General Practice in 1992 was a response to growing concerns about the possible demise of general practice, its fragmented organization, cost escalation and quality and financial accountability (Bailie et al. 1998; Marjoribanks and Lewis 2003; Pegram, Sprogis, and Buckpitt 1995). Divisions were responsible for allocating a mix of program funding, practice and service incentives, and contract and outcome-based funding linked to reportable activities (Rogers and Veale 2000a; Scott and Coote 2010). With reference to the typology of policy instruments devised by Lascoumes and Le Galès (2007), these agreement and incentive-based instruments were intended to mobilize policy actors (in this case Divisions and GPs) to achieve clinical and organizational performance objectives around population health.

Yet evaluations of the initial impact of the Division PHCO showed the power of professionals as policy actors in controlling the implementation space and resisting constraints on autonomy. Uptake of population health activities was largely influenced by what was measurable and consequently, population health outcomes that were difficult to define or attain in the short-term (e.g. mental health and access) were avoided (Rogers and Veale 2000a, 2000b). As a result, the Australian government introduced the National Quality and Performance System in 2005. This linked Division funding to national indicators of quality improvements and population health and a system of peer review and audits (DoHA 2004; Gardner, Sibthorpe, and Lonstaff 2008; McDonald et al. 2007). However, in recognition of the power of the profession, the Divisions were involved in development of the framework (Gardner, Sibthorpe, and Lonstaff 2008). As such, this performance system was consistent with 'de jure and de facto standard instruments' as described by Le Galès (2011, 21) as it featured a much more scientific and technical approach and was based on a degree of cooperative negotiation and execution (Lascoumes and Le Galès 2007). Furthermore, this period of reforms showed a strong preference for combining several different instruments as part of a non-interventionist mode of governance (Lascoumes and Le Galès 2007).

Still, the combination of policy instruments did not yield the expected population health results. For example, despite $3.0 billion expenditure since 1998 on one of the largest incentive schemes, the Practice Incentive Program (PIP), Cashin and Chi (2014) argued that it had failed to impact performance in the sector. In essence, they argued that the PIP payments were a motivation to seek accreditation and this became a proxy for outcomes (Cashin and Chi 2014). It could be argued that the discretion of Divisions to mediate between government and GPs as to what activities were pursued allowed them to take control and avoid coercion (Kassim and Le Galès 2010). Furthermore, in a market-based sector, the incentive-based schemes could be viewed as 'structures of opportunity' (Kassim and Le Galès 2010, 4), more so than generators of performance reform. In this case, there was concern about incentives creating business opportunities rather than higher standards of care (Webber 2012). Financial incentives were likely generating more clinical activity due to the potential for new sources of income without necessarily changing performance.

Medicare locals as an alternative PHCO in performance governance

A central point of difference between the Division PHCO and MLs was the notion of and rationale for population health performance. In contrast to the divisional form, the new governance structure manifested in MLs constructed population health performance as an interdisciplinary, partnership activity (Davies 2010; Sturmberg 2011) and the performance rationale as a community and public responsibility (Donato and Segal 2010). There was an expectation that MLs would facilitate working partnerships between GPs, established local hospital networks and other services to generate population health performance (Nicholson et al. 2012). MLs would also afford the opportunity to experiment with payment methods, including commissioning of services (Davies 2010; Donato and Segal 2010). This was decidedly different to the decades of agreement and incentive-based instruments which targeted front-line professionals and clinical activity.

A further contrast from the former Division PHCO was the stronger theme of transparency and accountability through public reporting of performance. The performance frameworks would be 'centralised and standardised, focussing on achievement against new performance standards' relating to access, quality, safety and financial and efficiency performance (DoHA 2011, 11). In this case, public reporting would be based on *Health Community Reports*[1] with comparison of MLs on key performance indicators. The rationale was that comparative representation of population health performance would enable improvements (DoHA 2011). Lascoumes and Le Galès (2007) would argue that these new information and communication instruments, which incorporated national standards and public reporting, constructed transparency and accountability through audience democracy. The assumption was that greater transparency would incentivize MLs to drive better outcomes for geographically based communities through general practice. However, these instruments would also implicate GPs and general practices in this population health performance, reinforcing their responsibilities to the public and funders.

The Australian Medical Association (AMA) was highly critical of a PHCO mode of governance that did not support the central role of GPs, or which interfered in the clinical matters of GPs (AMA 2010). MLs were viewed from within the profession as a tool to disenfranchise GPs and their key clinical role of patient care (Mountain Mar 2011). A review into MLs commissioned by the Minister of Health after the change of government in 2013 concluded that they disempowered GPs, imposed onerous administrative and contract conditions, were highly variable in focus and performance, and reporting requirements were complex, burdensome and relied on input and process measures providing little meaningful data in terms of population health performance (Hovarth 2014). Indeed, the lack of access to significant and reliable practice data other than Medicare fee-for-service data was seen to be a major hurdle in performance information and monitoring (Hovarth 2014). MLs were replaced with PHNs in July 2015. Early in the implementation, Leeder (2015) proposed that PHNs would not be dissimilar to MLs. Population health performance remained a central goal with performance measurement to incorporate national, local and organizational tiers of performance, with the intention that this would be made public.[2] There are two features to note, however. First, the objective is that PHNs will evolve into commissioning models, which suggests a stronger agreement-based approach. Second, there is a markedly enhanced role for GPs in decision-making in this new PHCO model (Leeder 2015), suggesting restoration of the more cooperative negotiation and execution of instrument implementation (Lascoumes and Le Galès 2007). At this opportune time in policy reform our study focused on a case study of MLs to elicit the performance rationalities and realities of the various professional, organizational and policy actors. The purpose was to examine how the various actors envisaged performance and the likely tensions surrounding population health performance and public reporting.

Case study

A case study of one purposively selected ML PHCO in Queensland, Australia, was the basis for a qualitative study of the perspectives of medical policy stakeholders, PHCO representatives and GPs. This case study was part of a larger two phase program of research on performance measurement, which included primary health care, schooling and higher education. Ethical approval was received from the university ethics committee. The aim of the ML case study was to explore how a performance focus on population health is imagined and might be mobilized by policy, organizational and professional actors. Over the two phases of the research program, a total of 28 policies, PHCO and professional participants were purposively recruited for the ML case study. Semi-structured interviews were conducted by two members of the research team over the period November 2011 to December 2013 to map the development and technologies of performance (phase 1) and to elicit the rationalities, realities and possible resistances of front-line professional perspectives (phase 2). In this paper, we explore the ways in which the professional and organizational positioning of GPs might be reconstituted with the broader concept of population health performance and the potential for the new performance approach to reshape the organizational and clinical domains. To do so, we draw on data from 13 participants including four medical and government policy participants at the strategic policy level, three organizational/PHCO representatives and six GPs. Once transcribed interviews were coded to broad, analytic dimensions of performance measurement using NVIVO. The resulting database was searched to identify and test linkages between performance measurement, reporting, government and the profession. Search results were subsequently categorized then tabulated (Miles and Huberman 1994) to enable further thematic analysis.

Results

The diverse rationalities on performance measurement, and the points of congruence and discord among the participants, were consistent with where their primary healthcare interests reside. The findings showed how rationalities of performance and contestation about accountability and quality differed within and across three levels of interests: (1) the consultation domain, which was a reference to professional autonomy and self-governance, and accountability to the patient; (2) the organizational domain where this autonomy was critical to private enterprise but evoked tensions about the priorities of practice-based population health more so than broader population health; and (3) the public domain, which was a reference to the rationale of public reporting of performance and contestation over the extent to which it undermined or reinforced trust in the consultation and organizational domains. In these ways, the analysis showed the different rationales at play and how different actors sought control of the policy space. The three main themes and sub-themes are discussed in the following section with representative extracts of participants[3] included to illustrate the themes.

The consultation domain: the 'good doctor' is accountable to the patient

There was general consensus among GP participants that the 'good doctor' is accountable to the patient within the consultation. This perspective was also somewhat evident at the strategic policy level but not at the organizational/PHCO level. For GPs, the one-to-one patient relationship regulated and legitimized their work. Accountability to the patient was also based on a professional rationale of self-governing 'to practice medicine ... to the best of my ability' (GP4) and to use patient and peer feedback as the benchmark for performance. This professional self-governance also legitimized professional practice standards and routines being judiciously adapted to the individual patient, rather than simply imposed in a standardized manner suggesting, 'it's a little bit more murky' in reality. (GP6)

> For me performance revolves around how well I practice medicine ... and the index of my performance to me is how well I have dealt with that problem with the patient ... That's a personal process, where one sets one's own standards. I think it's quite demanding, in terms of self-awareness and the ability to appraise one's own practice, and also revolves around patient feedback on their condition, specialist feedback on any referrals that are made and appraisal of patient health. (GP4)

Although there is explicit acceptance of the 'good doctor', accountable to the patient at the strategic policy level: 'Obviously they will work in the manner, which maximizes benefits for their patients' (SP3), there is also some caution about the potential bureaucratic encroachment of the ML bureaucracy on the 'good doctor'.

> We represent doctors who like to behave in an efficient manner, responsive to the needs of their patients, to be independent and accountable to their patients and free to the maximum extent possible, of bureaucracy and red tape. (SP1)

There is some contestation about new information and communication instruments being imposed outside of the professional quality framework and the 'push now about the management of data' (PHCO2). GPs spoke about the strictness of regular accreditation and auditing with data 'monitored quite stringently' (GP2). As a result, some GP participants were resistant to a new 'plethora of administrative bumph [impacting] my normal consultation process' (GP4), viewing this as an attempt to intrude on self-governance. Others wrestled with increasing intrusion into the 'closed-door consultation process' (GP5) while accepting the change to accountability.

> So then when they wanted to come in and actually access your personal ways of doing things ... I was very resistant to that ... it was the whole invasion of that private patient-doctor thing ... I'm not as bad about that now because it's the way of the world you know. (GP6)

The challenge of implementing new performance logic through the ML PHCO was evident from all perspectives. For GPs this revolved around their clinical role and resistance to intrusion. This might have been anticipated by the PHCO as there was some recognition of the need to maintain traditional incentive-based instruments to engage GPs in the new performance agenda.

> I think without too much intrusion, if we could be part of a process of looking at ... where there are gaps and needs within our consultations and within our patients' communities I think we'd be happy to as GPs generally to be part of that process. (GP5)
> There was a lot of opposition to the Medicare Locals taking that funding over from practices, a lot of opposition. So I guess in order to try and keep relationships strong and invest in local GP practices ... it kept them being supported in that way through the incentive program. (PHCO2)

There is a policy expectation that ML, as a meta-instrument, will enable traditional governance mechanisms to work more effectively (Kassim and Le Galès 2010). Yet, the rationale to make 'primary care more transparent ... to focus upon population health measures' (SP3) will need to harmonize with the notion of the 'good doctor' based on a taken-for-granted assumption and trust that GPs are self-governing professionals, motivated by professional values and norms. Whether this is achievable given the autonomous nature of the market-based organization of general practice was also dominant theme in the analysis.

The organizational domain: the performance enterprise

Most GPs extrapolated from accountability to the individual patient to accountability to 'our practice and our population'. This echoed the enterprise of general practice and further, the meaning of performance in a market context. The majority of GP participants were focused on what was happening with their individual patients and consequently, their practice population, not the 'broader population in a health perspective' (GP5). They linked accountability to individual patients to this notion of practice-based population health: 'the influence on population health comes in our practice from what we do with the individual' (GP4). However, there was some awareness of a broader population health perspective to inform general practice work 'with the people that you're dealing with' (GP1).

> Population-wise I have an idea about what's happening with my personal patient population, but not necessarily with the whole population. But then again, maybe I need to be right about my population. (GP1)

This perspective of performance whereby the focus of GPs was primarily on the patients of the practice was the proxy for broader population health. This recognized at the policy level (SP3), though the expectation is 'accountability back to their communities' (SP4). This was consistent with the PHCO perspective: 'performance measures are what difference we're making to the health of our region' (PHCO1).

The GP interest in organizational level data was motivated by both professional and business rationalities. GP participants were interested in such data but more so for professional self-governance and to support a financially viable practice. For GPs, information about organizational performance was particularly significant for identifying opportunities for improvements in a competitive environment. Consequently, there was some resistance to performance measurement instruments being imposed by the PHCOs.

> When you have a small practice like mine we actually find it's more important to look at what we assess [as] our own performance here rather than actually looking at performance outcomes of areas, regions … it's irrelevant to my practice. (GP3)
> Obviously, we're run as a business … and so that means we need to measure our performance in a whole range of areas to just make us viable and allow us to stay open … the data I have is very useful to me, maybe it's not so useful to everyone and … maybe the data that everyone else has isn't so useful to me". (GP2)

The enterprise environment of general practice drew different concerns about information and performance data for broader purposes. For one GP, data were there 'to help you manage the patient' (GP1), not for statistical purposes. Some GPs and policy participants raised concerns about data ownership and use of data, given the expectation the GP 'has a lot of reporting requirements, reports that they have to give [the PHCO]' (PHCO3).

> There are a huge number of barriers to [quality information]. The biggest one is that the data [are] owned by the practice and … not uniform [between practices]. There's no obligation to share your data with anyone and there's no quality consistency expected of that. (GP1)

Participants agreed on the challenge of implementing new performance instruments. One was the quality of data and an acceptance of 'a phase of fairly rough data' (GP1). The bigger challenge concerned the corporatized nature of general practice, including devising indicators given the diversity of the private enterprise where it is not 'just small and large practices … you get really niche practices … so getting indicators that are specific is a challenge' (SP2). Even so, for one policy participant the ability to control these private businesses to work towards population health was a significant hurdle.

> But basically [general practices] are private companies. So the amount of control or levers we have over them is fairly limited in that they are free to behave and work in the manner that they see fit. (SP3)

This theme highlighted the complexity of devising meaningful performance measurement in the context of professional self-governance and organizational complexities of practice-based population health. Furthermore, it suggested the power of professionals to invalidate instruments that do not align with these realities (van der Geer, van Tuijl, and Ruttle 2009). Consequently, publicly reporting performance was a particular source of contestation.

Public domain: representative performance

The policy expectation of MLs was for 'good accountability measures and giving confidence to the public' (SP3). The PHCO perspective was that new instruments, including the Heath Communities Reports, would provide an 'opportunity to report good news stories' (PHCO1). However, there were divergent views among the participants at all levels about the representation of population health performance through public reporting and the data on which these representations were based. Some GPs were skeptical about the capacity of government or the PHCO to accurately represent the complexity of clinical activity and population health. The subjectivity of the data capture and interpretation were other concerns.

> I am not strongly opposed to the principle that people ... should be able to look at comparative information across practices ... I remain to be convinced about the tools that are being used to collect that data ... all the measurements are very vague and not specific and very much depends on the observer and the treating doctors (GP3). Then [the government complains] that there is no review item numbers being used and then they say therefore it's not being reviewed. Of course it is being reviewed ... But the item number is not being charged. So analyzing what's happening with the rebate item number isn't really telling you what's going on. (SP1)

The skepticism about the representation and utility of performance data created some resistance among some GP participants and reluctance to embrace the new instrument logic of reportable population health performance. The PHCO participants sensed the importance of 'trying to form relationships ... recognizing what's priority to them but then adding on the broader activities involved' (PHCO1). However, unlike the Divisions approach, for GPs and some policy participants, see this process as 'top-down' and less consultative.

> I guess that if there was more input from general practitioners in formulating those kind of targets and support as well rather than just having a big stick approach where if you do the right thing we reward you if you don't then you're closed down, I think that would be good. (GP2)

There is ambivalence about whether the PHCO and public reporting was a trusted source of performance and feedback. Traditionally trusted sources included peer feedback and professional self-regulation processes: 'education from people I respect and good data that's put out ... I still have difficulty in somebody from Medicare Local coming in and giving ... education' (GP6). As a result, there was distrust about the 'validity of any comparison that's up on screen between different practices' (GP5) and limitations of instruments to capture the composite trusted sources of GPs.

> I don't think survey instruments can do it and for proper professional evaluation, personal opinion must come into it and personal evaluation. (GP4)

Consequently, professionalism and private enterprise created some uncertainty about whether the new type of PHCO and new information via public reporting could influence behaviour, and drive population health performance.

> But the general practice which has all your patient data and all the little things that are very critical can get some highly sophisticated indicators that by interpretation and interpreting by implementing actually has a positive outcome itself ... Can Medicare Locals actually do anything about it? Well actually no. They have to go to the practices to do something about it. (SP2)

Implicit in this theme were the challenges of information-based instruments designed to develop stronger transparency and accountability through 'audience democracy' demonstrated through public representation of performance data (Lascoumes and Le Galès 2007). In this case, professionals did not trust public reporting, derived through broad based top-down processes, to appropriately represent complex clinical processes or to effect change. The policy point was whether this new instrument could incentivize and effect population health performance in any discernible way.

Discussion

The new form of PHCO structure and new information and communication approach, including a raft of new population health performance measures and public reporting, are intended to enhance primary healthcare performance. This exploration of one ML PHCO provides a valuable insight into the implementation challenges of new instruments. These new policy instruments extend, or are designed to work alongside existing incentive-based instruments, albeit with other agreement-based approaches. However, as these findings show, overall these reforms have generated uncertainty and contestation. For the most part this centers on control of the policy space. Consequently, the findings highlight the precariousness of this new form of PHCO to engage GPs at the local level and the wider difficulty in steering primary healthcare services in the achievement of population health objectives within a market model.

A number of considerations about implementation of new policy instruments in the Australian context derive from these findings. First, policy reform in this area cannot ignore the strength of professional self-governance based on a professional identity and professional community. The strength of a shared professional identity and professional community is 'produced and reproduced through occupational and professional socialization by means of shared and common educational backgrounds, professional training and by membership of professional associations' (Evetts 2003, 401). In our study, performance based around accountability to the patient is embedded in medical knowledge, expertise, and peer group professional standards. The Divisions upheld this self-governance while negotiating improved organizational performance (Scott and Coote 2010) and arguably were a powerful vehicle in guarding professional practice and autonomy (Muzio and Kirkpatrick 2011).This helps to explain some of the ambivalence about the new form of PHCO among GP participants, particularly if seen to have a different concept of performance and rationale. As Marjoribanks and Lewis (2003) have revealed about previous reforms, the simultaneous uncertainty but potential of new instruments to coerce GPs are likely to challenge what it means to be a professional and generate resistance to control over practice issues.

Second, the extent to which new policy instruments unbalance the delicate equilibrium of co-existing rationales of professional work is also worthy of consideration. Freidson (2001) described the organizing frameworks and institutional logics of medical practice as rational–legal bureaucracy, market and professional work, which can both co-exist and compete. Still, there is likely to be a dominant logic, as McDonald et al. (2013) have observed, which means change is dependent upon the emergence of a new logic as the dominant form. The GPs interviewed in this study were motivated by both professional and business rationalities. They expressed high standards of self-regulation and performance, with reference to accreditation and audit that was also linked to both patient outcomes and practice viability. It is reasonable to suggest that the divisional structure helped negotiate any possible tensions herein since they had an acceptable disciplinary logic to accountability and performance improvement (Fournier 1999). In contrast, the idea of new information instruments attached to the MLs is to reposition professionals in a new social contract, reliant more on GPs and general practice working within an externally imposed bureaucratic framework of public reporting. Yet this need not threaten the dominant professional logic. As McDonald et al. (2013) have shown, reforms in England to alter the dominance of medical professionalism with a broader population health paradigm are not resisted if they build on existing professional and business logics rather than trying to control professional work.

In this case, although public reporting is argued on the basis of greater accountability and a high-performing sector, there is concern about the quality and provision of information. Consequently, this raises a third consideration of obligations and responsibilities and the extent to which meaningful information is achievable in the sector. As Lascoumes and Le Galès(2007, 15) have discussed, the notion of an audience democracy and citizens' rights of access to information sets up obligations to provide information and puts the onus on the holders of information to provide it whether in the public or private sector. In this case, population health performance is the frame used to coerce private providers to contribute the information. Yet GPs in this study do not legitimize this source of performance information for either the clinical and practice level. Further, the findings suggest that the difficulties around ownership of data by private practices will need to be resolved to engage GPs.

A fourth consideration concerns the representation of complex clinical work and the trustworthiness of public performance information. The GPs were particularly concerned about trustful information sources. The PHCO and policy participants also acknowledged the challenges of quality measures and capture of data. Professionals are generally wary of the difficulties of fully accounting for the complexities of clinical processes and problems with interpretation and comparison of data drawn from diverse clinical and organizational domains (Jorm and Frommer 2011). As Sturmberg (2011) has cautioned, there is danger in simply reducing problems in primary health care to failures of command and devising bureaucratic solutions that make assumptions about human behaviour in response to policy change.

Conclusion

An important feature of successful PHCOs internationally is 'the engagement of GPs in health planning, resource allocation and broader health system decision-making in a way that is consistent with their own professional aspirations and in the direction of wider health system goals of public health' (Donato and Segal 2010, 616). Despite the shift to PHNs, there are likely to be ongoing challenges and contestation about population health performance as primary healthcare governance. With reference to Power's (1999, 105) observations on auditing instruments in medicine, the issue will be whether the new PHCO instrument can harmonize the inherent power and control struggles between medical professionals and emergent managers (in this case PHCOs) and more so, organize GPs around a concept of population health performance that goes beyond audit accountability. This will depend, as history attests, on identifying the optimal combination of policy instruments to drive population health performance.

Notes

1. http://www.nhpa.gov.au/internet/nhpa/publishing.nsf/Content/Our-reports.
2. http://www.health.gov.au/internet/main/publishing.nsf/Content/phn-performance.
3. GP participant (GP1–6); PHCO participants (PHCO1–3); and Strategic policy participant (SP1–4).

Disclosure statement

No potential conflict of interest was reported by the authors.

Funding

This work was supported by the Australian Research Council Discovery Project Program under Grant (DP110100803). The views and opinions expressed therein are those of the authors and do not necessarily reflect those of Australian Research Council.

References

AMA. 2010. "AMA Response to Medicare Locals Discussion Paper on Governance and Function." Australian Medical Association.

Bailie, Ross, Beverly Sibthorpe, Bob Douglas, Dorothy Broom, Robyn Attewell, and Clare McGuiness. 1998. "Mixed Feelings: Satisfaction and Disillusionment among Australian GPs." *Family Practice* 15 (1): 58–66.

Britt, Helena, Graeme C. Miller, Joan Henderson, Clare Bayram, Lisa Valenti, Christopher Harrison, Ying Pan et al. 2014. *A Decade of Australian General Practice Activity 2004–2005 to 2013–2014*. Sydney: Sydney University Press.

Cashin, Cheryl, and Y-Ling Chi. 2014. "Australia: The Practice Incentive Program." In *Paying for Performance in Health Care: Implications for Health System Performance and Accountability*, OECD, World Health Organization, 109–126. Buckingham: McGraw-Hil, Open University Press. http://dx.doi.org.ezproxy.library.uq.edu.au/10.1787/9789264224568-en.

Coote, William. 2009. "General Practice Reforms, 1989–2009." *Medical Journal of Australia* 191 (2): 58–61.

Davies, Philip K. 2010. "Divisions of General Practice: Will they Transform or Die?" *Medical Journal of Australia* 193 (2): 75–77.

DoHA. 2004. *Divisions of General Practice: Future Directions: Government Response to the Report of the Review of the Role of Divisions of General Practice*. Canberra: Department of Health and Ageing.

DoHA. 2011. *Medicare Locals: Guidelines for the Establishment and Initial Operation of Medicare Locals & Information for Applicants Wishing to Apply for Funding to Establish a Medical Local.* Canberra: Department of Health and Ageing.

Donato, Ronald, and Leonie Segal. 2010. "The Economics of Primary Healthcare Reform in Australia - Towards Single Fundholding through Development of Primary Care organisations." *Australian and New Zealand Journal of Public Health* 34 (6): 613–619.

Duckett, Stephen, and Sharon Willcox. 2011. *The Australian Health Care System*. South Melbourne: Oxford University Press.

Dunbar, James. 2011. "When Big isn't Beautiful: Lessons from England and Scotland on Primary Health Care Systems." *Medical Journal of Australia* 195 (4): 219–221.

Evetts, Julia. 2003. "The Sociological Analysis of Professionalism: Occupational Change in the Modern World." *International Sociology* 18 (2): 395–415.

Fournier, Valerie. 1999. "The Appeal to 'Professionalism' as a Disciplinary Mechanism." *Social Review* 47 (2): 280–307.

Freidson, Eliot. 2001. *Professionalism: The Third Logic.* Chicago: University of Chicago Press.

Gardner, Karen, Beverly Sibthorpe, and Duncan Lonstaff. 2008. "National Quality and Performance System for Divisions of General Practice: Early Reflections on a System under Development." *Australian and New Zealand Health Policy* 5 (8): 1–8.

van der Geer, Eric, Harrie van Tuijl, and Christel Ruttle. 2009. "Performance Management in Healthcare: Performance Indicator Development, Task Uncertainty, and Types of Performance." *Social Science & Medicine* 69 (10): 1523–1530.

Hovarth, John. 2014. Review of Medicare Locals. Barton: Report to the Minister for Health and Minister for Sport.

Jorm, Christine, and M. Frommer. 2011. "Government Plans for Public Reporting of Performance Data in Health Care: The Case for." *Medical Journal of Australia* 195 (1): 40.

Kassim, Hussein, and Patrick Le Galès. 2010. "Exploring Governance in a Multi-level Polity: A Policy Instruments Approach." *West European Politics* 33 (1): 1–21.

Lascoumes, Pierre, and Patrick Le Galès. 2007. "Introduction: Understanding Public Policy through its Instruments – From the Nature of the Policy Instruments to the Sociology of Public Policy Instrumentation." *Governance: An International Journal of Policy, Administration, and Institutions* 20 (1): 1–21.

Leeder, Stephen. 2015. "Fiddling with Health." *MJA InSight*. Accessed July 24, 2015. https://www-mja-com-au.ezproxy.library.uq.edu.au/insight/2015/14/stephen-leeder-fiddling-health.

Le Galès, Patrick. 2011. "Policy Instruments and Governance." In *The SAGE Handbook of Governance*, edited by Mark Bevir, 142–160. London: SAGE.

Marjoribanks, Tim, and Jenny Lewis. 2003. "Reform and Autonomy: Perceptions of the Australian General Practice Community." *Social Policy & Medicine* 56 (10): 2229–2239.

McDonald, Ruth, Sudeh Cheraghi-Sohi, Sara Bayes, Richard Morriss, and Joe Kai. 2013. "Competing and Coexisting Logics in the Changing Field of English General Medical Practice." *Social Science & Medicine* 93: 47–54.

McDonald, Julie, Gawaine Powell Davies, Jacqueline Cumming, and Mark Fort Harris. 2007. "What can the Experiences of Primary Care Organisations in England, Scotland and New Zealand Suggest about the Potential role of Divisions of General Practice and Primary Care Networks/Partnerships in addressing Australian Challenges?" *Australian Journal of Primary Health* 13 (2): 46–55.

Miles, Mathew B., and A. Michael Huberman. 1994. *Qualitative Data Analysis: An Expanded Sourcebook*. 2nd ed. Thousand Oaks: Sage.

Mountain, David. Mar 2011. "Medicare Locals – Why they must be Opposed." *Medicus* 51 (2): 2–3. Accessed July 22, 2015.

Muzio, Daniel, and Ian Kirkpatrick. 2011. "Introduction: Professions and Organizations – A Conceptual Framework." *Current Sociology* 59 (4): 389–405.

Nicholson, Caroline, Claire Jackon, John E. Marley, and Robert Well. 2012. "The Australian Experiment: How Primary Health Care Organizations Supported the Evolution of a Primary Health Care System." *Journal of the American Board of Family Medicine* 25 (Suppl. 1): S18–S26.

O'Connor, Debra, and Chris L. Peterson. 2002. "General Practice in Australia: The Effects of Reforms and the Process of Privatisation." In *Health Policy in Australia*, edited by Heather Gardner and Simon Barraclough, 246–260. South Melbourne: Oxford University Press.

Pegram, Robert, Arn Sprogis, and Jeff Buckpitt. 1995. "Divisions of General Practice: A Status Review." *Australian Health Review* 18 (4): 78–94.

Power, Michael. 1999. *The Audit Society: Rituals of Verification*. Oxford: Oxford University Press.

Rogers, Wendy, and Bronwyn Veale. 2000a. "Dollars, Debts and Duties: Lessons from Funding Australian General Practice." *Health and Social Care in the Community* 8 (5): 291–297.

Rogers, Wendy, and Bronwyn Veale. 2000b. "*Primary Health Care and General Practice: A Scoping Report.*" Adelaide: Flinders University of South Australia.

Scott, Anthony, and William Coote. 2007. "Whither Divisions of General Practice. An Empirical and Policy Analysis of the Impact of Divisions within the Australian Health Care System." *Medical Journal of Australia* 187 (2): 95–99.

Scott, Anthony, and William Coote. 2010. "Do Regional Primary-care Organisations Influence Primary-care Performance? A Dynamic Panel Estimation." *Health Economics* 19: 716–729.

Sturmberg, Joachim. 2011. "Primary Health Care Organizations – Through a Conceptual and Political Lens." *Journal of Evaluation in Clinical Practice* 17: 525–529.

Webber, Tony. 2012. "What is Wrong with Medicare?" *Medical Journal of Australia* 196 (1): 18–19.

Hitting the target without missing the point: New Zealand's immunisation health target for two year olds

Esther Willing

ABSTRACT

The use of health targets as a form of performance measurement has become more prominent internationally as governments have sought to control public expenditure, produce greater efficiency and improve accountability. However, health targets have faced criticism for their potential to produce negative outcomes within a health system. This paper examines how a health target was used as a policy instrument within the New Zealand health system to improve immunisation coverage at two years of age. It explores how the immunisation health target was implemented within four case study sites and discusses the effectiveness of the health target as a policy instrument for improving immunisation coverage and addressing persistent immunisation inequities. Measuring and monitoring performance towards the immunisation health target improved accountability for immunisation coverage within the New Zealand health system and focused attention on improving immunisation coverage in a way that previous policy attempts had failed to do. Health targets may be an effective policy instrument for creating change within specific areas of a health system if their potential for dysfunctional consequences are taken into consideration at the outset.

Introduction

The phrase 'hitting the target, but missing the point' (Bevan and Hood 2006, 517) is often quoted when discussing health targets and their potential to create dysfunctional consequences within a health system. This paper presents research on New Zealand's immunisation health target for two year olds as a policy experience where local organisations were able to hit the target without missing the point. The immunisation health target for two year olds improved accountability for immunisation and focused attention on improving immunisation coverage in a way that previous policy attempts had failed to do. This paper argues that health targets may be an effective policy instrument for creating change within specific areas of a health system if their potential for dysfunctional consequences are considered at the outset.

The paper is divided into six sections. The first section outlines some of the key arguments for and against the use of health targets within the performance measurement literature. The second describes the New Zealand health system and the organisations involved in implementing the immunisation health target. The third outlines the immunisation health target within the context of immunisation policy in New Zealand, and describes immunisation coverage at two years of age over time. The fourth section summarises the methods that were used to explore the implementation of the immunisation health target within the New Zealand health system. Findings are presented in the fifth section focusing on the immunisation health target as a policy instrument for improving immunisation coverage. The final section discusses the key lessons that we can take from this policy experience.

Health targets as a policy instrument

Health targets are a form of performance measurement that have become more prominent as governments have sought to control public expenditure, produce greater efficiency and improve accountability (Bevan and Hood 2006; Mays 2006). However, there has been ongoing debate within the literature around their effectiveness as a policy instrument.

Advocates for the use of health targets have emphasised their ability to concentrate policy attention and improve health system performance (Smith and Busse 2010; Hood 2012). They claim that governments can use health targets to provide leadership and strategic direction within a health system (Campbell and Gibson 1997). As a policy instrument, health targets can focus attention and this focused attention can improve accountability for achieving policy goals. They can also create a structure for measuring and monitoring performance and this can improve the collection of data and its use for intelligence purposes (Hood 2012).

However, critics of health targets have argued that they can produce dysfunctional consequences that can have a negative effect within a health system (Bevan and Hood 2006; Radin 2006; Smith and Busse 2010). Perhaps the most prominent example of this was the gaming of the health target for emergency department waiting times within the English National Health Service (NHS), where patients were kept in ambulances and parked outside of hospitals until the emergency department was ready to receive them (Bevan and Hood 2006). Health targets can also lead to effort substitution as the focused attention on the health target can divert attention away from other important areas that need to be addressed but are perhaps more difficult to measure (Smith and Busse 2010).

The debate around the effectiveness of health targets as a policy instrument highlights their potential to create both positive and negative effects within a health system. But it is important to remember that all policy instruments produce specific effects outside of their stated objectives (Lascoumes and Le Gales 2007). The key for policy-makers is to understand the potential effects a health target might have within a health system and apply them to areas where they will improve performance without creating dysfunctional consequences.

Despite the extensive debate on the use of health targets within the literature, there are few examples where the use of a health target has improved performance with limited dysfunctional consequences on the wider health system. This paper seeks to address this gap in the literature by describing the use of a health target to improve immunisation coverage at two years of age within the New Zealand health system.

The New Zealand health system

The New Zealand health system provides universal access to health services to the New Zealand population and is largely funded by the government through taxation. The Ministry of Health is responsible for providing leadership as well as managing and developing the health system. The health system itself is structured around 20 District Health Boards (DHBs) that are responsible for providing or funding the provision of health services within their region (Ministry of Health 2013).

DHBs are geographically defined and are governed by a board of 11 members. Up to four of these members, including the chair and deputy chair, are appointed by the Minister of Health. The remaining seven members are publically elected every three years during local government elections. DHBs are contracted by the Ministry of Health to purchase and provide health and disability services for their populations and are funded based on the size and characteristics of their population.

Public hospitals are owned and funded by their respective DHBs and the majority of secondary health care services are provided directly by the DHBs. Primary health care services however are delivered through privately owned or not-for-profit general practices that are members of collective groups called Primary Health Organisations (PHOs). PHOs support the provision of primary health care services through general practices to people who are enrolled with that PHO. They receive capitation funding from the DHBs based on the number and characteristics of their enrolled population and as they are not geographically defined, their general practices may be located across more than one DHB.

The majority of immunisation services in New Zealand are delivered at the general practice level of the health system. The DHBs contract the PHOs to deliver immunisation services to their enrolled population through their general practices. At the time of this research, children under six received free or mostly subsidised health care. Immunisations on the National Immunisation Schedule were provided free of charge to all children.

Immunisation records are entered and stored on an electronic information system called the National Immunisation Register (NIR). The NIR was introduced by the Ministry of Health in 2005 and allows health professionals to access and record accurate information on a child's immunisation history, even when their family has moved or changed their general practitioner. Data are entered on the NIR by practice nurses and each DHB has an NIR coordinator who is responsible for ensuring that the information is up to date and entered correctly at the general practice level.

Immunisation coverage at two years of age

Increasing immunisation coverage to 95% at two years of age had been a policy objective within the New Zealand health system for almost two decades (Ministry of Health 2003). And yet, immunisation services remained fragmented and there was very little accountability for immunisation coverage at both a national and local level. This contributed to low rates of immunisation coverage and significant immunisation inequities between Māori children (Māori are the indigenous people of New Zealand) and non-Māori children (Grant et al. 2010). Such low rates of coverage and persistent immunisation inequities led to reoccurring outbreaks of vaccine-preventable diseases such as pertussis, measles, mumps and rubella (Turner et al. 2000).

In 2007, the Ministry of Health set a health target for immunisation that 95% of two year olds would be fully immunised by July 2012. The immunisation health target was part of 10 national health targets that were introduced to 'provide a greater focus for action and lift health system performance in priority health and disability areas' (Ministry of Health 2008, 5). No new funding was allocated for the implementation of the health targets and DHBs were expected to achieve the immunisation health target within their existing funding and resources.

Almost two years later, a change of government saw the incoming Minister of Health revise the original set of health targets down to six health targets and place stronger emphasis on accountability to both central government and the public (Tenbensel 2009). While some of the original health targets were abandoned and others revised, the health target for immunisation remained the same.

Measuring and monitoring progress towards the immunisation health target

Immunisation coverage at two years of age was calculated at both a national and local DHB level every three months. A child was considered fully immunised if they had received all of the scheduled immunisation events before their second birthday. Data from the NIR were used to monitor progress towards the immunisation health target over time and the Ministry of Health also published these data in national and local newspapers to create public accountability for achieving the health target.

National level of immunisation coverage

When the immunisation health target was introduced in 2007, the national rate of immunisation coverage at two years of age was measured at 67%. Over the course of the immunisation health target experience, immunisation coverage at two years of age increased from 67% to 93% when the health target ended in June 2012 (see Figure 1). While the

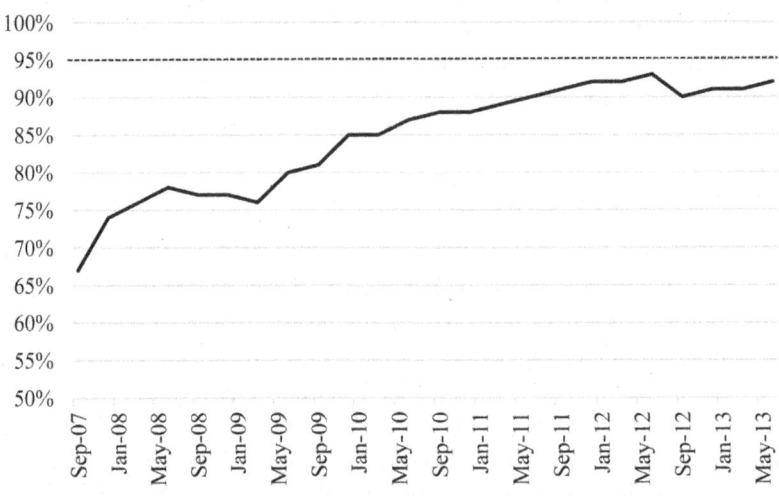

Figure 1. National level of immunisation coverage at two years of age.

rate of immunisation coverage at the national level failed to achieve the health target of 95%, this was a significant improvement considering the inability of previous policy attempts to increase immunisation coverage within the New Zealand health system.

Immunisation inequities by ethnicity

There were significant immunisation inequities between children from different ethnic groups when the health target was introduced in 2007. While rates of immunisation coverage were relatively comparable among New Zealand European and Asian children (at 74% and 73%, respectively), rates of immunisation coverage were much lower for Māori and Pacific children (at 59% and 63%, respectively). There were also immunisation inequities for children within the 'other ethnicity' category, which included all children enrolled on the NIR of any ethnicity other than New Zealand European, Māori, Pacific or Asian.

Over the course of the immunisation health target experience, rates of immunisation coverage increased for all ethnic groups. When the health target ended in June 2012, Asian and Pacific children had the highest rates of immunisation coverage (at 98% and 97%, respectively). The rate of immunisation coverage for New Zealand European children was 93% and immunisation coverage for Māori children was 92%. Children within the 'other ethnicity' category had the lowest rate of immunisation coverage at 87% (see Figure 2).

Immunisation inequities between Māori and non-Māori children

Immunisation coverage for Māori children had increased from 59% in September 2007 to 92% in June 2012. And the level of immunisation inequity between Māori and non-Māori children had reduced from 11% to 1% at the national level (see Figure 3). At the local level, immunisation inequities between Māori and non-Māori children were eliminated within some DHBs. In terms of health policy and indigenous health outcomes, this is an important achievement as Māori experience significant health inequities when compared to non-Māori New Zealanders (Bramley et al. 2005; Harris 2007).

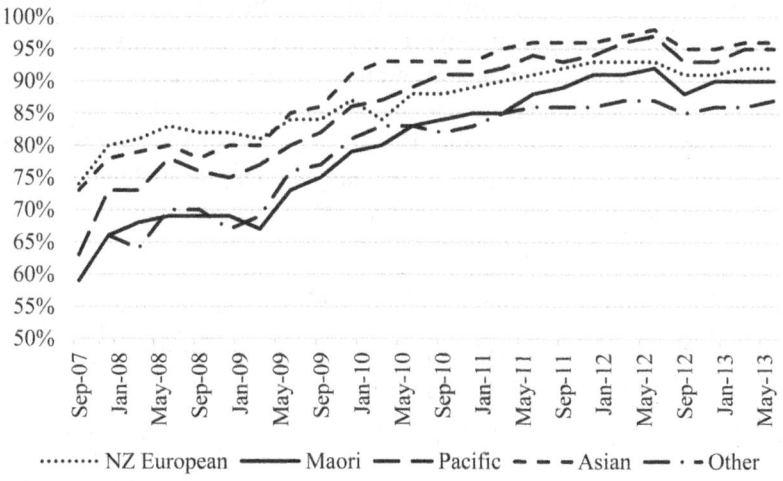

Figure 2. National level of immunisation coverage at two years of age by ethnicity.

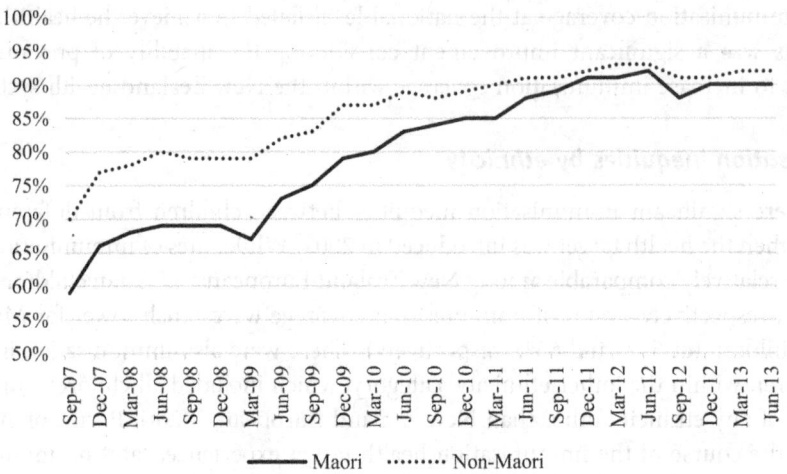

Figure 3. National level of immunisation inequity between Māori and non-Māori children at two years of age.

The immunisation health target improved immunisation coverage at two years of age in a way that previous policy attempts had been unable to achieve. But how did this change occur?

Methodology

This research used a case study methodology to explore how the immunisation health target for two year olds was implemented at the local level within four DHBs. A case study methodology allowed the researcher to examine how these DHBs responded to the health target as a policy instrument, and what actions they took to improve immunisation coverage within their regions.

Four DHBs were selected as case study sites based on two dimensions of performance (see Table 1). The first dimension that was considered was performance towards the immunisation health target at the time of selection in June 2010. The DHBs that were eventually selected included one high-performing DHB, one low-performing DHB and two DHBs that had steadily improved immunisation coverage tares within their region over the course of the health target experience.

The second dimension of performance that was considered was the level of immunisation inequity between Māori and non-Māori children. This limited the selection of case study sites to DHBs located in the North Island of New Zealand as the DHBs in the South

Table 1. Case study sites along two dimensions for performance.

	Low level of immunisation inequity between Māori and non-Māori children	High level of immunisation inequity between Māori and non-Māori children
High performance towards the health target	Hawke's Bay DHB	
Improving performance towards the health target	Waikato DHB	Auckland DHB
Low performance toward the health target		Bay of Plenty DHB

Island have much smaller Māori populations. The 15 DHBs in the North Island were evaluated on their level of inequity in immunisation coverage between Māori and non-Māori children. This dimension of performance facilitated the selection of two DHBs with relatively low levels of immunisation inequity and two DHBs with high levels of inequity between Māori and non-Māori children.

Two phases of semi-structured interviews were conducted within each of the four case study sites to allow the researcher to capture the experiences of key informants involved in the implementation of the health target as well as their reflections on the implementation process after the health target for two year olds had ended. Key informants were recruited through professional networks from the national Immunisation Advisory Centre.

The first phase of interviews focused on collecting information on the implementation process for the immunisation health target from multiple perspectives within each case study site. An interview schedule was developed from the literature and questions focused on: the local systems and processes in place for immunisation services before the health target was introduced; how these had changed to improve immunisation coverage and address the health target; the relationship between different organisations working towards the health target, and the impact of measuring and monitoring performance towards the health target.

Key informants included individuals responsible for child health and immunisation within the DHB planning and funding team, managers within the PHOs located in each case study site, Public Health Physicians responsible for immunisation within the region, the NIR coordinators within the region and the Immunisation Coordinators who worked between the PHOs and the primary care providers at the local level. Thirty-three interviews were conducted across the four case study sites over a five-month period between August and December 2011. Interviews lasted between 45 minutes and 1 hour in length and were conducted at a location convenient for the key informant.

The researcher also interviewed the national immunisation health target champion within the Ministry of Health in November 2011. This provided a national perspective on the implementation of the immunisation health target and the extent to which policy learning occurred between different DHBs.

The second phase of interviews revisited some of the key informants within each case study DHB. These key informants were selected by the researcher based on the rich information that they had provided in the phase one interviews and included individuals working in the DHB Planning and Funding team, managers within the local PHOs and the Immunisation Coordinators. Sixteen interviews were conducted across the four case study sites during a two-month period from September to October 2012. These interviews took place three months after the end date of the health target and allowed the key informants to reflect back on the implementation process. This perspective was useful because the interviewees were in a position to discuss what they thought had worked, or had not worked, during the implementation process. The researcher was also able to validate themes that had been identified during the analysis of phase one interviews with the key informants.

Interviews were recorded and transcribed by the researcher. Interview data were analysed using a deductive thematic analysis approach that drew upon the literature. A coding matrix was developed using the literature and research questions and this was applied to a sample of four interviews to refine the coding process and produce a coding matrix that could be utilised across all of the interviews. Phase one interviews were coded and analysed before phase two interviews were conducted and informed the interview schedule for the phase two interviews. Phase two interviews were coded using the same coding matrix and then analysed by the researcher. The research findings presented here focus on the immunisation health target as a policy instrument.

Research findings

This section presents the research findings under the following themes: improving accountability for immunisation coverage, measuring and monitoring performance towards the health target, creating a hierarchy of immunisation champions, funding and resources to improve immunisation services, dysfunctional consequences of the health targets and an overview of what happened after the health target ended.

Improving accountability for immunisation coverage

Before the immunisation health target was introduced there was very little accountability for immunisation coverage within the New Zealand health system. Immunisation services were seen as the responsibility of primary care and coordination of these services within the health system was fragmented (Turner et al. 2000).

The immunisation health target clearly identified immunisation at two years of age as a key government priority. This focused attention on immunisation and improved accountability for immunisation coverage within the health system. Key informants across all four case study sites talked about the way in which the health target highlighted immunisation at two years of age as a national and local priority.

> It became a priority and we had competing priorities ... but we were able to elevate immunisation as one of the key priorities, one of the top priorities, and I think that helped. (Interview with Bay of Plenty DHB Planning and Funding, November 2012)

The health target also identified DHBs as the organisations responsible for improving and maintaining high rates of immunisation coverage within the health system. This shifted responsibility for immunisation coverage from the individual level of primary care providers to the regional level of the DHBs. This shift in accountability was an essential factor that contributed to the success of the health target as a policy instrument. It required the DHBs to take a leading role in improving local systems and processes for immunisation. DHBs were well placed to oversee the implementation of the immunisation health target as they were responsible for contracting immunisation services on behalf of their population and could take a systems perspective to improving immunisation coverage.

> We've always had relationships with other providers. I think probably we've been stronger about saying you have to deliver, if you have a contract with us this is what we expect you to deliver and being really much more focused. (Interview with Waikato DHB Planning and Funding, October 2012)

Measuring and monitoring performance towards the health target

Previous policy attempts to improve immunisation coverage within the New Zealand health system had failed as the government was unable to measure and monitor immunisation coverage. The newly established NIR allowed the Ministry of Health to accurately measure immunisation coverage at both a national and local level.

> If it weren't for the NIR, we couldn't have done this health target. (Interview with Auckland DHB Planning and Funding, September 2011)

The Ministry of Health used data from the NIR to measure the level of immunisation coverage within DHBs and at a national level for all children turning two years of age during that three-month period. Measuring and monitoring performance towards the immunisation health target focused attention on immunisation and improved accountability for immunisation coverage.

There were no financial incentives or penalties tied to the immunisation health target. Instead, hierarchical accountability for the health target was reinforced by the involvement of the Minister of Health when DHBs failed to meet the target set for that quarter. The Minister of Health would contact the CEOs of these DHBs to discuss how the DHB would improve their performance during the next quarter.

> I think that having the Minister sitting behind it is really critical, because if you know that there isn't anything particular happening around a particular issue, he will actually go straight to the Chief Executive and have a conversation. (Interview with the Ministry of Health Immunisation Health Target Champion, November 2011)

This pressure from the Minister of Health on DHB senior management was highly effective and elevated the immunisation health target as a key priority within the DHBs.

Published league tables to compare DHB performance

The Ministry of Health also created league tables comparing DHB performance against one another at the end of each three-month period. These league tables were published in national and local newspapers to improve accountability to the public in terms of progress towards each of the health targets. The media attention that followed the publication of these league tables played an important role in motivating DHBs to improve their performance towards the health target.

> I think having the health targets and the way the Minister publishes them now, that's really focused the DHB. (Interview with Bay of Plenty DHB PHO Manager, November 2012)

For DHBs that were high performers, the league tables gave key informants a sense of validation and encouraged them to improve on and maintain high rates of immunisation coverage in their region. While for DHBs that were performing poorly, the league tables held an element of 'naming and shaming' (Bevan and Hood 2006) as key informants talked about the pressure coming from DHB management to improve their ranking.

Collegial competition

One of the consequences of the published league tables for the immunisation health target was that it created an element of collegial competition between organisations across each level of the New Zealand health system. All of the case study DHBs stated that they were very aware of their position on these league tables relative to the other DHBs and that they were a strong motivator for improving their level of immunisation coverage.

However, this element of competition did not prevent DHBs from sharing what had worked for them with other DHBs around the country. The underlying values of protecting children from vaccine-preventable diseases and improving population health ensured that competition did not stifle communication and collaboration between DHBs. Instead it created a culture of collegial competition between DHBs, where they were competing against one another but also supporting and encouraging one another to improve their performance.

> I think there's always been a willingness to share across the country, that's never been an issue, even though we were sort of competing with each other, we always liked to look at our rankings, but there's never been a problem with people sharing whatever has worked for them. (Interview with Bay of Plenty DHB Planning and Funding, November 2012)

At the local level, this culture of collegial competition was evident between PHOs within the case study DHBs. PHOs were aware of their level of performance relative to other PHOs in their DHB; however, they also recognised that performance towards the health target was measured at the DHB level. This required them to work together to improve immunisation coverage across all of the PHOs in their region.

A number of PHOs replicated this element of collegial competition by publishing their own league tables on a monthly or quarterly basis comparing the performance of their primary care providers against one another.

> Each practice can see how they're going in relation to their little population, so they know and they know what their peers are doing as well, so they can see if they are falling behind. It's quite powerful. (Interview with Waikato DHB PHO Manager, October 2011)

One PHO that was involved in this research openly named their primary care providers, while others anonymised their league tables so their providers could review their performance relative to other providers in the PHO, but could not identify the other primary care providers. Primary care providers who were performing poorly were forced to recognise their performance was not at the same level as other providers in their PHO and that they needed to improve their systems and processes for immunisation. And the PHO was able to take what had worked within high-performing providers and share these experiences with the providers that needed to improve their performance towards the health target.

Creating a hierarchy of immunisation champions

When the health target was introduced, the Ministry of Health required each DHB to identify an immunisation champion who was responsible for overseeing the health target within their region. In some DHBs this involved recognising an informal champion for immunisation who was already in place. While in other DHBs this required the DHB to identify an individual within the DHB to take on the immunisation champion role. The concept of immunisation champions was developed further within the case study DHBs as they identified their own immunisation champions within their PHOs.

> Identifying the target champion was a real core feature that had to happen, even though it was a scary thing initially. And actually ensuring that there is an equivalent person in each DHB and hopefully within each PHO as well, so giving a sort of hierarchy of champions

nationally, district level and locally, and that actually bred success. (Interview with the Ministry of Health Immunisation Health Target Champion, November 2011)

By the final year of the health target experience (July 2011–June 2012), this hierarchy of immunisation champions had become well established and reinforced the vertical dimension of accountability for the immunisation health target, from the Ministry of Health at the national level down to the immunisation champions within the DHBs, their PHOs and the primary care providers at the local level. It is also improved communication between central government and organisations at the local level.

Funding and resources to improve immunisation services

While two of the DHBs involved in this research did invest additional funding and resources to address the health target, there was no additional funding from central government associated with the immunisation health target. These DHBs needed to allocate additional funding to immunisation services in their region.

> I think it makes it [the DHB] very focused on wanting to achieve a target and getting that. It also means that the DHB does put the funding in to that area to try and achieve the target. So I do think it does make a difference. (Interview with Waikato DHB Planning and Funding, October 2012)

The other two DHBs involved in this research did not invest additional resources. Instead, they reallocated existing resources for immunisation services and were able to use them more efficiently.

> Well we had absolutely no new funding, so what we had is what we had. (Interview with the Hawke's Bay DHB Immunisation Coordinator, October 2012)

There was a pre-existing performance payment within primary care for achieving high rates of immunisation coverage and this performance payment continued to be paid to primary care practices through their PHOs. The Ministry of Health aligned the performance criteria with the health target but this payment focused on primary care providers, not the wider implementation of the health target within a DHB.

Development of immunisation networks

As a policy instrument, the immunisation health target acted as a catalyst for change at the local level. It required local organisations who were involved in delivering immunisation services to come together and work in a way that previous policy attempts to improve immunisation were unable to achieve. All of the case study DHBs developed immunisation networks that were able to focus on addressing the immunisation health target within their region.

> It wasn't organised as a system within our DHB, it was contracting out, contracting out, so bringing that all together ultimately and that didn't have to be the colocation one business model, so the [immunisation network] meeting was a way of fixing that with a number of different players. (Interview with Auckland DHB Planning and Funding, October 2012)

These immunisation networks met on a regular basis and this improved communication between the organisations involved as individuals were able to discuss local challenges to the implementation process and negotiate how these challenges would be addressed. Regular meetings also nurtured the sense of a team approach towards the immunisation health target and improved ownership of the health target across multiple organisations at the local level.

> We need to work together. Not for me or you, but for the population we serve. There is now more sharing of knowledge and information. (Interview with Bay of Plenty DHB PHO Nurse Manager, September 2011)

Dysfunctional consequences of the health target

Within the literature on health targets there has been much debate about the dysfunctional consequences that health targets can have within a health system (Bevan and Hood 2006; Hood 2007; Smith and Busse 2010). Their use within the English NHS drew attention to the potential for subversive behaviour and gaming of a target that impacted on wider health system performance and health outcomes for patients (Bevan and Hood 2006).

Within the New Zealand experience of the immunisation health target there was no evidence of gaming of data used to measure and monitor performance towards the health target. This was due in part to the way that information was recorded on the NIR, as monitoring the immunisation health target used data drawn directly from the individual immunisation records of New Zealand children. These immunisation records were updated at the primary care level and entering inaccurate information or changing information on these records had strong ethical implications in terms of privacy laws in New Zealand. One way to avoid the gaming of data could be to centralise the collection of data while still allowing that data to be accessed and used by organisations at a local level.

Another prominent criticism of health targets is that they can cause effort substitution by focusing attention on the target area at the expense of other important areas that need to be addressed but are perhaps more difficult to measure (Smith and Busse 2010). Determining whether effort substitution occurred due to the immunisation health target was difficult as immunisation was already a core service within the New Zealand health system. This research had no way of tracking what was not done due to the focus on the health target.

One area where effort substitution was evident was the way in which the health target focused attention on immunisation coverage at two years of age, overshadowing immunisation coverage rates across all of the other ages that were measured.

> Because we've focused on the health target, all the work that's gone into improving immunisation rates at two years, and we haven't had the same effort going into improving immunisation rates at six months, and twelve months, and eighteen months and five years. So yes, you might have good figures for two years, but our figures for the other rates are still a lot lower than they should be. And that's the flip side to it, yes you focus attention on the health target but you're not capturing the whole spectrum of immunisation work. (Interview with Bay of Plenty DHB Planning and Funding, November 2012)

Addressing the immunisation health target also required sustained effort from organisations and the individuals working within them and this led to target fatigue during the final quarters of the health target experience.

> We kind of got really intense on that last quarter, everything got more intensified ... everything was like we've got one more quarter to go, let's ramp it up. (Interview with Bay of Plenty DHB Immunisation Coordinator, November 2012)

Key informants stated that they were exhausted when the health target for two year olds ended in June 2012 and this target fatigue was reflected in the drop in immunisation coverage at two years of age during following quarter.

After the health target ended

After the health target ended in June 2012, immunisation coverage at two years of age reduced from 93% in June 2012 to 91% in June 2013 (refer to Figure 1). Pressure to achieve the health target was relieved, but the Ministry of Health continued to measure and monitor immunisation coverage at two years of age as part of their routine monitoring programme for DHBs. Three years after the immunisation health target for two year olds ended, the national level of immunisation coverage for two year olds remained high at 93% for the quarter ending in September 2015 (Ministry of Health 2015). This is a significant achievement considering the low rates of immunisation coverage before the health target for two year olds was introduced.

The policy experience of a health target to improve immunisation coverage does not end there though. When the immunisation health target for two year olds ended in June 2012, the Ministry of Health replaced it with a new health target for immunisation which stated that '95% of babies would be fully immunised by eight months of age by December 2014'. This gave DHBs three months to follow up on the immunisation event that is scheduled for five months of age. It was a shorter timeframe than the health target for two year olds, which had given the DHBs nine months to follow up on the immunisation event scheduled at 15 months.

While this research did not examine the new health target, key informants involved in this research anticipated the health target shifting to focus on the younger age group before it happened. They stated that the new eight-month health target would shift the focus away from immunisation coverage at two years of age and that this could lead to a reduction in immunisation coverage at this age. But they also emphasised that achieving high rates of immunisation coverage at eight months of age would theoretically make it easier to achieve high rates of immunisation coverage at two years of age.

> If we get things going well at eight months then ultimately they'll eventually become our two year olds, so things should be improving. But I wouldn't be surprised if there is going to be some deterioration in the two year old target, but we're still looking at them, we're still trying to get them up to date just before they turn two. (Interview with Waikato DHB Planning and Funding, October 2012)

Discussion of policy learning

Internationally there is increasing interest around ways governments can improve health system performance without investing additional funding. The immunisation health target demonstrates that a health target can be used to improve health system performance in a specific area without additional funding from central government. However, to avoid situations where organisations are 'hitting the target, but missing the point' (Bevan and Hood

2006, p. 517), policy-makers need to carefully consider how performance towards a health target will be measured and monitored.

The immunisation health target was measured and monitored using a national surveillance system that made it very difficult for DHBs to game data. It allowed the Ministry of Health to accurately measure levels of immunisation coverage within each DHB and use these data to compare performance towards the health target across the country. It also measured and monitored levels of immunisation coverage by ethnicity, which ensured that immunisation inequities were highlighted for attention. DHBs and PHOs were also able to draw upon these data for their own organisational learning and this aspect of the NIR helped DHBs to improve their local systems and process for immunisation.

Within the literature on performance measurement, one of the potential challenges in using ranking systems such as league tables is that they can focus attention on the organisations at the top and the bottom of league table, allowing organisations to hide in the pack (Carter, Klein, and Day 1992). However, as DHBs were expected to achieve the health target as a minimum level of performance the focus was on achieving the health target rather than hiding in the middle of league table.

The use of league tables to compare DHB performance also created an element of collegial competition that motivated DHBs and PHOs to improve their performance while also encouraging them to share policy lessons with each other. Health professionals work within a collegial environment where individuals from different professions need to cooperate to provide health services within their communities. An element of competition can motivate health professionals to improve organisational performance within a specific area while still maintaining an egalitarian culture of cooperation (Hood 2012).

However, it is also important to consider the impact that sustained effort towards a health target and the stress associated with this focused attention will have on the individuals involved as well as the culture of the organisation. For this reason, health targets should be used over a set period of time and once they have ended they should be replaced with ongoing monitoring (Le Grand 2007). The immunisation health target had an end date of July 2012 and this focused the energy and effort of health professionals involved in delivering immunisations services. Although there was a small decrease in immunisation coverage at two years of age once the health target had ended, levels of immunisation coverage have remained high and continued to be measured and monitored by the Ministry of Health.

Conclusion

The use of health targets as a form of performance measurement has become more prominent internationally as governments have sought to control public expenditure, produce greater efficiency and improve accountability. The New Zealand immunisation health target experience demonstrates that health targets may be an appropriate and effective policy instrument for improving health system performance in a specific area. But policy-makers need to consider their potential to create dysfunctional consequences within the wider health system if they want to ensure that organisations hit the target without missing the point.

Disclosure statement

No potential conflict of interest was reported by the author.

Funding

This research was funded by a University of Auckland Doctoral Scholarship.

References

Bevan, G., and C. Hood. 2006. "What's Measured Is What Matters: Targets and Gaming in the English Public Health Care System." *Public Administration* 84 (3): 517–538.
Bramley, D., P. Hebert, L. Tuzzio, and M. Chassin. 2005. "Disparities in Indigenous Health: A Cross-Country Comparison between New Zealand and the United States." *American Journal of Public Health* 95 (5): 844–850.
Campbell, H., and A. Gibson. 1997. "Health Targets in the NHS: Lessons Learned from Experience with Breast Feeding Targets in Scotland." *British Medical Journal* 314 (1030): 1–7.
Carter, N., R. Klein, and P. Day. 1992. *How Organisations Measure Success: The Use of Performance Indicators in Government*. London: Routledge.
Grant, C., N. Turner, D. York, F. Goodyear-Smith, and H. Petousis-Harris. 2010. "Factors Associated with Immunisation Coverage and Timeliness in New Zealand." *British Journal of General Practice* 60: e113–e120.
Harris, R. 2007. *Hauora: Maori Standards of Health IV*. Wellington: Te Ropu Rangahau Hauora a Eru Pomare.
Hood, C. 2007. "Public Service Management by Numbers: Why Does It Vary? Where Has It Come from? What Are the Gaps and Puzzles?" *Public Money and Management* 27 (2): 95–102.
Hood, C. 2012. "Public Management by Numbers as a Performance-Enhancing Drug: Two Hypotheses." *Public Administration Review* 72 (S1): 85–92.
Lascoumes, P., and P. Le Gales. 2007. "Introduction: Understanding Public Policy through Its Instrument – From the Nature of Instruments to the Sociology of Public Policy Instrumentation." *Governance: An International Journal of Policy, Administration and Institutions* 20 (1): 1–21.
Le Grand, J. 2007. *The Other Invisible Hand*. Princeton: Princeton University Press.
Mays, N. 2006. *Use of Targets to Improve Health System Performance: English NHS Experience and Implications for New Zealand*. Wellington: New Zealand Treasury.
Ministry of Health. 2003. *Immunisation in New Zealand: Strategic Direction 2003–2006*. Wellington: National Immunisation Programme, Ministry of Health.
Ministry of Health. 2008. *Health Targets: Moving Towards Healthier Futures 2007/08 – The Results*. Wellington: Ministry of Health.
Ministry of Health. 2013. Overview of the Health System. Accessed July, 2013. http://www.health.govt.nz/new-zealand-health-system/overview-health-system.
Ministry of Health. 2015. National and DHB Immunisation Data. Accessed January 2016. http://www.health.govt.nz/our-work/preventative-health-wellness/immunisation/immunisation-coverage/national-and-dhb-immunisation-data.
Radin, B. 2006. *Challenging the Performance Movement: Accountability, Complexity and Democratic Values*. Washington, DC: Georgetown University Press.

Smith, P., and R. Busse. 2010. "Targets and Performance Measurement." In *Performance Measurement for Health System Improvement: Experiences, Challenges and Prospects*, edited by P. Smith, E. Mossialos, I. Papanicolas, and S. Leatheran, 509–536. Cambridge: Cambridge University Press.

Tenbensel, T. 2009. National health targets revised. In *Health Policy Monitor.* http://www.hpm.org/survey/nz/a14/1.

Turner, N., M. Baker, J. Carr, and O. Mansoor. 2000. "Improving Immunisation Coverage: What Needs to Be Done?" *New Zealand Public Health Report* 7 (3/4): 11–14.

The challenge of quantifying national well-being: lessons from the *Measures of Australia's Progress* initiative

Cosmo Howard and Amber Chambers

ABSTRACT
In recent decades, the use of gross domestic product (GDP) as a proxy for national well-being has been criticised on the grounds it excludes important social and ecological considerations. Several alternatives have been proposed that promise to generate more comprehensive and balanced quantitative measures of well-being, but all of these alternative indicators remain contested and controversial. This paper critically reviews Australia's contribution to this effort: the Australian Bureau of Statistics' (ABS's) Measures of Australia's Progress initiative. Unlike many other alternatives to GDP, the Australian initiative does not settle on one measure but uses expert-mediated public consultation to establish a 'dashboard' of indicators. In so doing, this model makes explicit the serious challenges confronting efforts to coherently define and measure progress in late modernity. In its attempt to integrate diverse views on national progress, the ABS has created an ambiguous tool that is not being taken up in public and political discourse.

1. Introduction

Measurement is an essential activity of the modern state. It has become a highly visible element of governing in recent decades. Influential neoliberal rationalities and new public management principles stress the need to track, audit, rate, rank and report 'performance' across almost every sphere of state activity. Increasingly, such 'calculative practices' (Miller, Kurunmaki, and O'Leary 2010) extend into civil society, where the intricacies of individuals' lives are observed and transmuted into 'headline indicators', which in turn inform public debate, policy decision-making and programme implementation. Critical scholars have suggested that these practices are increasingly ubiquitous and hegemonic, and that formerly unquantified aspects of governmental performance and social life are progressively succumbing to regimes of enumeration (Higgins and Larner 2010; Latour 1993).

In this paper we explore a prominent component of the contemporary push to extend measurement into formerly unquantified domains, namely, the move to create more comprehensive measures of national or social 'well-being', 'development' and 'progress'. The conventional and long-established measure of national well-being, gross domestic product (GDP), has been widely criticised for neglecting important elements that cannot be straightforwardly counted, such as environmental conservation, subjective happiness and the quality of governance (Bates 2009; Schepelmann, Goossens, and Makipaa 2009; Schwartz 2010). Efforts to move beyond GDP accelerated in the 1990s as public and political support for post-industrial and post-material values (favouring individual rights, social equality, environmental sustainability and 'quality of life') grew (cf. Stiglitz, Sen, and Fitoussi 2010). Statisticians and economists pondered how to incorporate a broader range of dimensions into a new headline societal indicator. Their efforts spawned numerous indicators, including the Human Development Index (HDI), Genuine Progress Indicator (GPI) and Happy Planet Index (HPI). These are clear examples of the extension of quantitative logics into previously unquantified domains, which use sophisticated statistical techniques to attach numerical values to seemingly intangible phenomena.

In this paper we ask: what are the challenges involved in developing new, more comprehensive measures of well-being that seek to assign quantitative values to formerly unquantified aspects of governmental performance and social life? We present a review of the Australian Bureau of Statistics' (ABS's) Measures of Australia's Progress (MAP) initiative. Whereas most efforts to find alternatives to GDP attempt to replace it with a substitute indicator, MAP follows a different path: it includes a wide range of measures that could be associated with 'progress', selected via expert-mediated public consultation processes. Furthermore, instead of trying to distil these measures into a single number, it presents a 'dashboard' of figures and leaves the user to draw their own conclusions about overall trends. Since the introduction of MAP in 2002, this dashboard approach has become increasingly influential, finding favour for example in the recommendations of France's 'Stiglitz Commission' (Stiglitz, Sen, and Fitoussi 2010). It has been implemented in the OECD's Better Life Index, launched in 2011.[1]

MAP has received very little scholarly attention to date. The key existing academic review of MAP criticises the ABS for failing to commit to a single coherent definition of progress, accusing the agency of timidity in the face of potential criticism (Davidson and Wilson 2011). We take a different approach and ask: what does MAP tell us about the *capacity* of state agencies to define and measure progress in 'late modernity'? We argue MAP is subject to the same constraints as all post-GDP measurements of well-being: there is little public consensus about what is required to improve well-being or produce 'progress', and there are also large 'data gaps' where no suitable indicator exists to measure potentially important aspects of progress. Unlike other alternative measures, however, MAP renders these problems explicit. By faithfully representing fragmented public views on the drivers of progress, MAP sheds light on just how difficult it is to determine what societal progress is. MAP seeks to acknowledge late-modern disagreement about progress with an inclusive definition, but in the process it teaches users that national progress is impossible to define coherently and impractical to measure.

This paper makes a contribution to existing critical literature on the politics of quantification and measurement by extending knowledge on state measurement processes. It suggests that existing research has been too quick to assume quantification is ubiquitous and hegemonic. Rather, quantification is fraught with dilemmas and confronts firm limits. Thus, states cannot arbitrarily impose centralized classificatory grids onto their populations in late modernity. At the same time, efforts to explicitly acknowledge definitional disagreements and to involve the public in measurement do not necessarily lead to greater credibility for and acceptance of official numbers.

We begin the article with a brief historical analysis of the idea of progress in the liberal democratic West. We show that progress was once taken for granted, but the notion is now deeply contested and distrusted. We then explore recent attempts to measure progress through alternatives to GDP, including criticisms of these efforts. The article then explains our review methodology briefly, followed by a discussion of the MAP case study findings. In the discussion we reflect on what these findings say about the politics of quantification by proposing three dilemmas that plague efforts to quantify governmental performance and social well-being in late modernity.

2. Defining progress

Efforts to measure progress imply that such a thing exists. So what is progress? In everyday talk the word can mean two things: movement towards a goal or destination (e.g. 'We have made good progress on our hike to the campsite'), and/or improvement of a specific circumstance or condition without a specified end point (e.g. 'Your knowledge of bread making techniques is progressing'). This article is interested in a particular type of progress: that associated with societies or nations. We therefore need to know: *what does it mean for a society or nation to progress?*

In this section we suggest that the concept of social or national progress has a long history in the Western world. Nisbett (1994, 4) suggests 'No single idea has been more important than, perhaps as important as, the idea of progress in Western civilization for nearly three thousand years'. We argue the definition of progress has moved through three stages in western liberal democracies: the *classical liberal* stage in which progress was assumed to be an external force driving changes in human society (Arendt 1973; Mannheim 1936); a *Keynesian* phase in which progress was assumed to require governmental management of the macroeconomy (Girvetz 1963; Jessop 1999); and the current *late-modern* phase, in which there is profound public disagreement about what constitutes progress. Here we briefly summarise each phase in turn, concluding that the literature on progress sees little hope for securing consensus on what progress means, for the foreseeable future.

The idea that societies undergo a gradual process of improvement is often attributed to the liberal political thought that emerged during the European enlightenment, beginning in the seventeenth century (Mannheim 1936). 'Classical liberals' saw progress as an inevitable historical force leading to a definite outcome: the 'emancipation of man' from ignorance and despotism (Bauman 2000; Beck 1992; Mannheim 1936). Advances in scientific knowledge would allow humans to control nature and turn it to their purposes:

> That the 'old' industrial society was obsessed with progress has often been emphasized ... the *latent* faith in progress ... the faith in the method of trail and error, the possibility of a systematic mastery of external and internal nature that was being gradually constructed. (Beck 1992, 200, emphasis original)

These ideas of inevitable historical progress were of course not confined to liberalism. They found expression, albeit in modified form, in Marxist ideas about the inevitability of a crisis of capitalism and its replacement with communism, as well as Christian millenarian views about the inevitability of a future period of blessedness (Mannheim 1936). The point here is that these 'early modern' views saw progress as a driving force – an invisible, powerful, unassailable cause of overwhelmingly positive changes in human society (Bauman 2000).

The late nineteenth century represented the high water mark of faith in progress as a benevolent driving force of history (Spadafora 1990). Events of the early twentieth century – two world wars and a global economic depression – did much to undermine the notion that increasing human knowledge, expanding industrial production and accelerating technological innovation would lead to a better life for all. In its place was put a new view of progress: something that was possible and desirable, but not inevitable. Progress had to be secured via deliberate policy action. Responsibility came to be laid in large part at the feet of new systems of *macroeconomic management*, built upon the ideas of John Maynard Keynes. He proposed that a free economy contained instabilities, but that these could be prevented from turning into depressions via careful use of corrective fiscal policy to stimulate sluggish economies and slow down overheating markets (Donaldson 1992). Avoiding economic stagnation became, in the words of President Eisenhower, a 'Great Crusade', and just as important to the well-being of the nation as military defence (Girvetz 1963, 355). Thus by the mid-twentieth century the notion that there was some natural, invisible driving force called progress that pushed societies towards general advancement came to be rejected (Galbraith 1958; Giddens 1991). Established in its place was the view that progress was possible, but only by conscious, deliberate, collective action. Progress in this 'high modern' era ceased to be an autonomous causal force and became a *potential outcome* of a properly managed, rationally guided and carefully monitored (measured) economic system.

Sociologists of 'late modernity' (Bauman 2000; Beck 1992; Beck, Giddens, and Lash 1994; Giddens 1991) argue the cultural assumptions and political interests that upheld the Keynesian paradigm of managed economic progress began to break down in the 1960s. The expansion of economic production came to be associated with pollution, species extinction and the destruction of natural amenities. Faith in the benefits of scientific discovery came into question as the health and ecological dangers of new chemical and nuclear technologies emerged (cf. Giddens 1991). The rise of green political and cultural movements drew attention to this and encouraged greater social appreciation for the natural world. Acceptance of the benefits of industrial progress has been partly replaced in advanced economies by a 'post-materialist' outlook that acknowledges trade-offs between material wealth and quality of life (Inglehart 1977). The prevailing paradigm of economic management and government interventionism came under challenge not just from environmentalists, but also in terms of its capacity to avoid economic stagnation and social insecurity. The credibility of interventionist Keynesian macroeconomic management was damaged by its seeming inability to address the chronic 'stagflation' of the 1970s, leading to the rise of new-right anti-government thinking in the 1980s (Hall 1993). Subsequent neoliberal discourse encouraged a decoupling of individual progress from national progress by suggesting individuals are responsible for their own well-being (Bauman 2000; Beck and Beck-Gernsheim 2002).

In late modernity, the meaning of societal progress is thus unclear. Gone is the classical liberal faith in the inevitability of progress. Gone also is the post-war optimism that progress is possible so long as government gets the 'policy settings' right. Bauman (2000, 133) concludes that the 'foundation of trust in progress is nowadays prominent mostly for its cracks, fissures and chronic fissiparouness'. At best we can say that there are now multiple, partly overlapping but partly conflicting ideas about what constitutes progress, and these ideas are based on different value sets and political interests.

3. Measuring progress

This section reviews historical and contemporary efforts to measure national or societal progress and highlights problems encountered in the measurement process. We suggest that the economic concept of GDP has for three-quarters of a century been a dominant (albeit de facto) measure of societal progress. In recent decades, critics have argued GDP is an inadequate measure of national well-being, development or progress, and have proposed a variety of modifications or replacements claimed to better measure national progress. However, as we shall see below, none of these 'alternative' measures of national progress have achieved general acceptance.

The concept of GDP was an outgrowth of the Great Depression and World War 2 (WWII). It formed a key element of Keynesian/New Deal approaches to handling stagnation, by focusing on monitoring the aggregate levels of economic growth and implementing macroeconomic policies to adjust these. Governments also used GDP to provide the public with evidence that they could sustain and provide adequate materials for fighting WWII whilst upholding sufficient manufacture of consumer goods and services (Marcuss and Kane 2007). GDP as a global measure of economic progress was strengthened in the 1940s. Following the war, GDP growth was seen as the key to 'creating lasting world peace' (Costanza et al. 2009, 5). As a consequence, GDP came to be treated, implicitly, as a measure of societal well-being and progress.

As we suggested in the previous section, critics have questioned the validity of the connection between economic growth and increased individual and societal well-being (Schwartz 2010; Talberth, Cobb, and Slattery 2007, 1). GDP is criticised for leaving out aspects of life that are not measured through the national accounts:

> These include failure to account for changes in natural resources and intangible capital (including human capital), nonmarket household production (with some exceptions), leisure, external costs and benefits associated with production and consumption, income distribution, economies of household size, social costs of unemployment, threats to national security, democratic rights, and restrictions on liberty. There are also problems associated with the measurement of government services, such as education and health. (Bates 2009, 5)

Criticisms of the inadequacies and exclusions of GDP have spurred attempts to find alternatives to GDP that better account for the full range of factors that influence wellbeing (Cobb, Halstead, and Rowe 1995a, 1995b; Daly 1996; Daly, Cobb, and Cobb 1989; Lawn 2003, 2005; Talberth, Cobb, and Slattery 2007).

Alternatives to GDP fall into three categories: adjustments, replacements and supplements (Schepelmann, Goossens, and Makipaa 2009). GDP adjustments rely on GDP but seek to add 'a variety of economic, social or environmental factors' so as to correct the GDP figure (Schepelmann, Goossens, and Makipaa 2009, 24). Examples include the Index of Sustainable Economic Welfare, GPI, Green GDP and Genuine Savings. Adjustment measures consider personal consumption, public non-defensive expenditures, private defensive expenditures, capital formation, services from domestic labour, the costs of environmental degradation and depreciation of natural capital (Lawn 2003). Conversely, replacements do not rely on GDP but seek alternative measures to establish well-being (Schepelmann, Goossens, and Makipaa 2009). Replacements include the HDI, Ecological Footprint, HPI, Gross National Happiness and the Environmental Sustainability Index. Supplements seek to provide additional data to be viewed alongside conventional GDP and include the National Accounting Matrix Environmental Accounts, German Environmental Economic Accounting and the MAP initiative (Schepelmann, Goossens, and Makipaa 2009).

All of these alternatives to GDP have been subject to criticism. Adjustments, replacements and supplements have been criticised on the grounds that it is difficult or impossible to assign a monetary value to socially constructed criteria such as environmental sustainability (Schepelmann, Goossens, and Makipaa 2009). Moreover, these alternative approaches to GDP are criticised for relying on data that is difficult or impossible to collect. Data reliability is a particular challenge for many developing countries, as the required data suffers from incomplete coverage, measurement errors and biases (Bagolin 2004). Supplement approaches such as MAP have been criticised for providing a smorgasbord of measures with little clarity on how each should be weighted, leading to an inability to provide assessments of overall progress (Davidson and Wilson 2011).

Despite the extensive effort that has been poured into developing alternatives to GDP, none has achieved the kind of taken for granted acceptance that GDP did in the past, or even does at present (Shergold 2011). The very fact that there are so many competing and overlapping efforts to develop such measures illustrates the lack of consensus on a model for measuring well-being or progress in late modernity.

4. Our study methodology

Our study involved a systematic, critical, qualitative review of the documentation surrounding the ABS's MAP initiative. We chose this initiative for two reasons. Firstly, it has not been the subject of significant critical analysis to date (but see Davidson and Wilson 2011; Saunders 2002). Furthermore, it is relatively unusual among alternatives to GDP in that it does not present a formal (quantitative) model of progress or well-being, but leaves the precise definition of progress open and relies on the user drawing their own independent conclusion(s) about overall progress based on a suite or 'dashboard' of indicators. In other words, the MAP initiative eschews the goal of capturing well-being in a single number.

In terms of the materials used as data for our critical textual analysis, we reviewed all of the major online and printed documentation surrounding the MAP initiative. This included biennial reports (Trewin 2002, 2004, 2006), MAP summary sheets (ABS 2013c), MAP feature essays (ABS 2012, 2013a, 2013c), articles written by the ABS about MAP (Trewin and Hall 2005) and MAP media releases (ABS 2004a). Importantly, we systematically reviewed the interactive online MAP 'dashboard', which presents the findings and conclusions on progress across the various dashboard indicators. We also reviewed the small number of scholarly articles about MAP (Davidson and Wilson 2011; Saunders 2002), including an ABS response to critiques (Sutton 2011). Our review of these materials was guided by an effort to understand the challenges MAP faces in measuring progress. We sought in particular to see how MAP defines progress and how it seeks to measure progress.

5. Measures of Australia's progress

MAP is the ABS's attempt to create a tool to answer a deceptively simple question: 'is life in Australia getting better?' (Trewin 2004). MAP has its origins in the mid-1990s, when ABS staff began considering how the agency should respond to new alternative measures of national well-being. The ABS felt that this was an extension of a long history of work measuring progress:

> Measuring progress – providing information about whether life is getting better – is perhaps the most important task a national statistical agency like the ABS undertakes. Measuring progress has been the responsibility of the ABS since colonial times. A national statistical agency like the ABS plays an important role in providing the indicators that allow assessments of progress to be made, by those who formulate and evaluate policy, by researchers and by the Australian community. (ABS 2013c)

Following the 1997 'Measuring Progress: Is Life Getting?' Better Conference (Eckersley 1998), the ABS decided to use a suite of indicators approach to create a 'dashboard' which would allow Australians to judge for themselves whether or not life in Australia was progressing (Trewin and Hall 2005). A major rationale for the choice of the dashboard approach was that attempting to combine diverse measures into a single index could lead to misleading and even meaningless results (Trewin and Hall 2005). This logic is neatly captured in the more recent report of the Stiglitz Commission:

> To take an analogy, when driving a car, a meter that added up in one single number the current speed of the vehicle and the remaining level of gasoline would not be of any help to the driver. Both pieces of information are critical and need to be displayed in distinct, clearly visible areas of the dashboard. (Stiglitz, Sen, and Fitoussi 2010, 17)

In developing the MAP suite of indicators, the ABS used an 'iterative' approach, in which it drew on expert advice and 'stakeholder' consultation to develop and refine a list of indicators. Despite making much of the 'wide ranging consultations' surrounding the choice of categories and indicators (ABS 2004a, 6, 8, 9), the ABS is vague in its publications about how the public was consulted. The ABS started by seeking the views of experts, distilled these into a framework of broad categories for measuring progress, then consulted with the public in 2001, prior to the release of the first MAP in 2002 (ABS 2004b; Trewin and Hall 2005).

A subsequent consultation exercise in 2011–2012 was undertaken to determine if the categories required updating. There is more detail about how these consultations were carried out (ABS 2012, 2013c). The ABS conducted a series of national and state/territory fora. Participants were almost entirely made up of 'key stakeholders' – governments and other data users such as academic researchers (ABS 2012). These fora were supplemented by a social media campaign soliciting the views of the general public. While the ABS at times frames MAP as a bottom-up consultative exercise designed to gather the authentic views of ordinary Australians on progress – 'you spoke, we listened' (ABS 2013c) – it is important to acknowledge that the consultation processes was not a simple exercise in ascertaining the unmediated views of the public. Instead, the process of designing categories of progress and choosing specific indicators in MAP has been heavily steered and shaped by the judgement of statistical experts, both external and internal to the agency.

A screen shot of the most recent dashboard page at time of publication is provided in Figure 1. As the key at the bottom of the figure shows, areas with tick/check marks have progressed, areas with tildes have not changed, and areas with crosses have regressed. Question marks designate domains without suitable data – so called 'data gaps'. The ABS accepted that stakeholders were likely to define progress in divergent ways, such that a consensus was unlikely. Hence, the aim of the dashboard was to be transparent

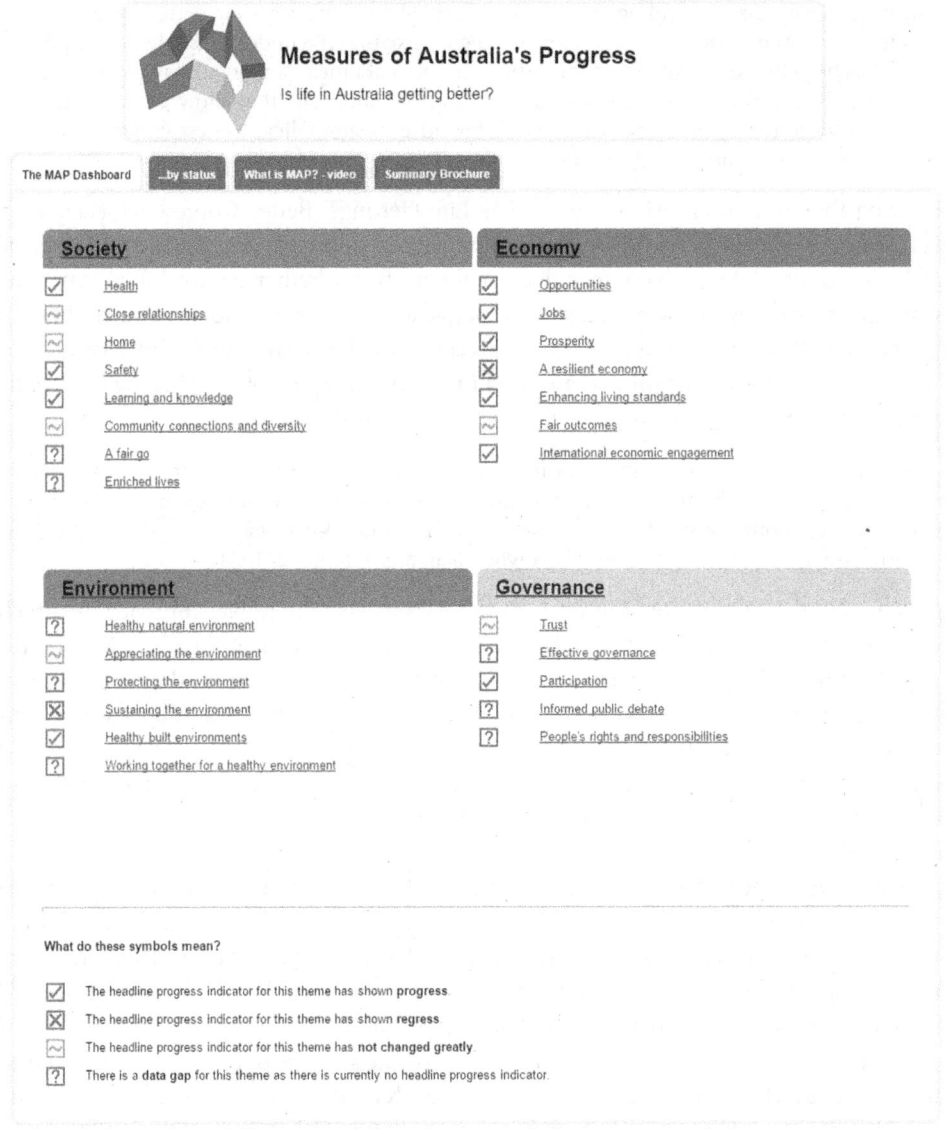

Figure 1. The MAP dashboard. Source: http://www.abs.gov.au/ausstats/abs@.nsf/mf/1370.0

and offer a broad picture or overview to the public, letting Australians decide how the country was doing in multiple areas (Trewin and Hall 2005).

Originally, MAP had three main focus domains: economy, society and environment. Fourteen aspects of the three domains were chosen to reflect the overall themes. Headline indicators measuring aspects of progress were chosen for each. In later MAP releases headline indicators were coupled with supplementary indicators in an attempt to present a more rounded picture of progress.

The headline indicator data, along with supplementary indicators and data taken from ABS reports, publications and online releases, was collated and simplified to make it digestible for the general public. In 2002, 2004, 2006 and 2010, a release of MAP was published demonstrating where progress or regress had occurred in the various domains. Adjustments were made with each release and by 2013, MAP had four main focus domains: economy, society, environment, and the new addition, governance and democracy. MAP publications have consistently emphasised the importance of dialogue and adaptation in the design of the initiative. The ABS accepts that MAP will change as public values change, but also expects that over time greater clarity will be achieved regarding the items to be measured (Sutton 2011; Trewin 2002; Trewin and Hall 2005).

How does MAP define progress?

Going by the initiative's title, MAP's creators believe progress exists and can be measured. So how did they move from the vague notion of 'life getting better' to a measurable construct of progress? MAP defines progress as follows:

> The model seeks to show progress as the unambiguous movement of society in a positive direction – that is, an improvement. Importantly, this idea of improvement implies there are aspirations (or end points) in mind that society is progressing towards, and that these need to be defined in order to know whether progress is occurring. (ABS 2012, 13)

Unlike the GPI and other alternatives to GDP, which define progress with a mathematical formula that weighs a specific number of quantified variables chosen by the measurers, the ABS's MAP approach explicitly recognises that progress can be defined in multiple ways, and that different individuals will have different views on what progress is. To this end the ABS asked experts and the public what they thought progress was. Following a process of 'refining' these views to distil key themes (ABS 2012), the ABS came up with a list of factors believed by the public to contribute to progress. These include, in the domain of *society*: health, the quality of close relationships, learning and knowledge, and 'enriched lives'; in the domain of *economy*: jobs, prosperity, fairness and international economic management; in the *environmental* area: healthy environment, appreciating the environment, sustainable environment and working together for a healthy environment; and in the area of *governance*: trust, effective governance, participation, informed public debate, and rights and responsibilities.

Thus, MAP does not provide a clear definition of what progress is. It relies on the opinions of a selection of members of the general public and experts about the factors that might make life better, but does not explain how or give precise details about what specifically has to happen with each factor for life to get better. Davidson and Wilson (2011, 47) argue the ABS's motive in keeping the definition vague was to 'avoid a perception of cultural or political bias', and that as a result the ABS has limited MAP's usefulness. The implication of this is that the ABS is being timid and should simply define and model progress properly and wear the inevitable criticism. However, by attempting to build a definition of progress via public consultation, MAP actually illustrates just how difficult defining and modelling societal progress is in late modernity. The challenge of defining progress is not just about avoiding controversy; it is also a fundamental ontological issue of deciding *what progress is*. MAP goes further in illustrating this point than other 'alternatives to GDP' precisely because it is so explicit about its assumptions and because its creators set out to represent the diversity of public views about progress.

How does MAP measure progress?

In addition to making the challenge of defining progress explicit, MAP also highlights the difficulty of measuring it. As we elaborate below, MAP shows that there are many areas of progress where no data of sufficient quality exists. Furthermore, where data does exist, its relation to the construct supposedly being measured is often highly problematic.

The challenges of finding measurements or statistics to signify progress stand out in the area of missing data on the MAP dashboard. Almost one-third – 8 of 26 – of the headline indicators of the MAP dashboard are marked as 'data gaps'. MAP documentation suggests that data gaps come in four types:

1. The concept is not yet developed enough to measure.
2. The concept is important for progress but may not lend itself to meaningful measurement.
3. There is no data of sufficient quality to inform on progress or
4. There is only one data point so a progress assessment cannot be made (ABS 2013c, 21).

For the most part, the ABS is optimistic that these data gaps will close in the future. Statements such as 'there is *currently* no headline progress indicator' (ABS 2013c emphasis added), 'for which there are no agreed statistical measures *yet*' (Trewin 2002, 5 emphasis added) and '[w]e will continue to explore options for a suitable indicator in the future' (ABS 2013c) suggest subtly and explicitly that the ABS expects to plug many of the gaps in the existing dashboard. The inclusion of items in the dashboard before appropriate data exists to measure them might even be interpreted as a way of supporting a claim for resources for new data collections to fill the gaps. At the same time, their inclusion is an explicit reminder that the ABS cannot find numbers to measure many of the things the public would like it to. Furthermore, the ABS is also forced to concede:

> Although the concept [being measured] is important for progress, it may not lend itself to meaningful measurement. This being the case, while we will continue to consider this area of progress, there is no guarantee that we will have a progress indicator for it in the future. (ABS 2013c)

Thus, the message explicitly delivered by MAP is that, despite the proliferation of quantitative indicators over the last century, when it comes down to measuring what the public want to measure, the ABS can only find data for just over two-thirds of the items. Furthermore, it may never be able to credibly quantify some of the drivers of progress.

The challenge of measurement is further reinforced in areas that are not data gaps. A good example is the MAP measure of 'participation', defined as: 'Australians aspire to have the opportunity to have a say in decisions that affect their lives'. The dashboard begins with the 'headline indicator' for participation. This is the number of Australians of voting age who are eligible to vote. The ABS justifies its choice of measure without recourse to references or research:

> Voter enrolment is an important part of the aspiration for participation in decision making and governance processes ... The proportion of eligible Australians enrolled to vote is considered a good measure of progress for participation in decision making and governance processes because it is a measure of people's participation in electing governments. When the proportion of eligible Australians enrolled to vote is high, it indicates that people in the community are engaged in determining the governments that make decisions that affect them. Voter enrolment in Australia is also heavily influenced by compulsory voting laws which should be accounted for when interpreting this indicator. (ABS 2013c)

The ABS then concludes participation has progressed:

> We have decided that the opportunity to participate in decision making and governance processes in Australia has progressed in the last three years because the proportion of eligible Australians enrolled to vote (our headline progress indicator for participation) has increased ... In 2013, 91% of eligible Australians were enrolled to vote. This is higher than the proportion three years earlier in 2010 which was 90%. (ABS 2013c)

Following this analysis, the dashboard reminds the reader that this is 'not the whole story' and references other indicators of participation. These include voter turnout in federal elections (this does not vary much in Australia where voting is compulsory and backed by fines), membership of civic and political groups (which happens not to have changed between 2006 and 2010) and responsibility, measured by the number of overseas born residents taking up citizenship.

These measures show the oversimplification required to measure complex constructs with numerical indicators. For example, many political scientists and sociologists reject the suggestion that voting enrolment is a good measure of participation. Many citizens take part in elections but do not wish to have any further involvement in political processes (Hibbing and Theiss-Morse 2002). Other citizens may reject conventional channels of participation such as voting while at the same time engaging in extensive 'sub-political' activity via social movements and online campaigns (Beck 1992). Furthermore, the suggestion that an incredibly complex and contested construct like 'responsibility' is captured by looking at applications for citizenship is also deeply problematic. For one thing, what does it mean to speak of 'progress' in the context of responsibility? Does it mean more people taking responsibility for their own lives? The chosen measure is also narrow. Applicants for citizenship make up a tiny proportion of Australian society. They probably apply for citizenship for a wide variety of reasons, and thus it is not at all clear why we should interpret the number of applications as saying something about the general state of responsibility in Australia.

The claim being made here is not that these are incorrect measures. Nor are we proposing superior alternatives. We accept that the ABS made a good faith effort to select valid and useful data. Nevertheless, these dashboard indicators draw the user's attention to the distance between complex social realities and existing numerical measures.

We have suggested that the ABS has deliberately avoided coming to overall conclusions about their measures of progress. However, there are occasions when the agency has tried to make general claims. Some examples of this are heavily qualified, such as this 2009 reflection on overall trends in the MAP findings:

> The headline indicators presented in MAP suggest some progress in the economic and social domains over the last decade. This article has illustrated some of the associated reinforcement between economic and social progress. While the environmental domain is more difficult to measure comprehensively, some of the headline indicators suggest that economic and social progress has come partly at the cost of negative environmental impacts. Nevertheless, there is some evidence of relative decoupling in recent years that has reduced the trade-off between economic growth and environmental degradation. Sustainability is important in this context, and international initiatives to develop indicators of sustainability currently underway may help inform the presentation of MAP indicators in the future. (ABS 2009)

In other cases, the ABS has been less restrained. For example, one of the agency's 2013 media releases, confidently entitled: *Is Australia progressing? The results are in*, makes a definitive argument about overall progress:

> ABS Director, Fiona Dowsley said 'The latest release of MAP shows us that overall, Australia is in pretty good shape with more progress or little movement, than regress, which is a great result. Progress was found in the areas of health, learning and knowledge, jobs, living standards and participation. We have only regressed in the areas of our economy's resilience and sustaining the environment' said Ms Dowsley. (ABS 2013c)

The implication is that various headline indicators are of equal weight, such that we can infer progress simply by subtracting the number of indicators that have gone down from those that have gone up. In effect, this media release made a powerful value judgement; namely that a decline in economic resilience and environmental sustainably is outweighed in importance by employment growth, better health and more learning. This is precisely what the ABS has tried to avoid through MAP. It reminds us of statisticians' powerful inclination towards making general, quantitative conclusions about complex social phenomena. Furthermore, the ABS appears to be operating with two inconsistent notions of progress: the late-modern notion that progress is contested and cannot be summarised, and the Keynesian idea that observations of national life can be tallied into a single metric of social progress.

6. Discussion

This article addressed the challenges facing efforts to expand measures of national progress to include formerly unquantified aspects of well-being. While the most prominent efforts try to replace GDP with a new single-number indicator, the approach taken by Australia's statistical agency explicitly communicates the divergence of views on progress and the difficulties of quantifying many components of national well-being. In this discussion we reflect on the implications of our findings for theoretical work on the politics of quantification and performance measurement.

As we have seen, existing theories of quantification and measurement stress the hegemony of numbers. According to this work, few realms of life that governments are interested in escape the 'statistical gaze' (Bödeker 2001). Those that do are progressively succumbing to the relentless drive for quantification embodied in the spread of performance measurement practices and the rapid expansion of 'big data' techniques (Mayer-Schönberger and Cukier 2013). Numbers are thus ubiquitous and authoritative, and powerfully shape behaviour.

In contrast, our work on MAP suggests firm limits to quantification. We conclude that these limits take the form of a series of interrelated *dilemmas*. The dilemmas are: coverage vs. rigour; detail vs. deployability; and consultativeness vs. comparability. These dilemmas are likely to confront any 'measurer' who seeks to quantify the impacts of policies and programmes on social well-being. We summarise these dilemmas in the remainder of this discussion.

Firstly, efforts to impose grids of quantification on government programmes and social life encounter problems of coverage: some areas have been extensively measured and others have not. This difficulty is made clear in the MAP initiative's explicit acknowledgement of numerous 'data gaps' in its suite of headline indicators. Yet in many cases the issue is not coverage per se, but *quality*. Data exists, but the statisticians have decided it does not conform to their quality standards. These standards exist and are enforced for two reasons: firstly, from the perspective of professional integrity, the measuring agency wishes only to release data that meets technical standards of rigour; and secondly, from the perspective of the measuring agency's public authority, the organisation must be careful not to release numbers that might be challenged and therefore threaten high levels of public trust in the broader statistical programme (see, for example, ABS 2010; Fellegi 1996; UNSD 2003). This illustrates the point that the authority of numbers, and the measuring agencies that produce them, is far from absolute. These arguments are consistent with work showing how governmental institutions in late modernity can no longer take their political authority for granted, but must constantly 'perform' legitimacy and guard against criticism, so as to maintain their credibility and influence (Hajer 2009). In this context, a statistical agency cannot simply present numbers and expect public acceptance.

Actors engaged in quantification thus face a dilemma as they seek to expand the coverage of their measurements. Do they secure their authority by demonstrating the comprehensive coverage of their data, or do they establish authority by restricting their claims to the narrow fields where their results meet the highest standards of rigour? In terms of the established critical literature on quantification and measurement, this dilemma suggests that those engaged in quantification do not enjoy hegemonic authority; rather, their work is subject to contestation and critique.

Secondly, measurers face a tough choice in deciding whether to make their indicators detailed or easily deployable by users. By 'deployable', we mean that users can efficiently utilise numbers for their own purposes, to inform decisions and support or challenge political arguments. MAP sought to be more detailed than other alternatives to GDP, by integrating an unusually wide range of plausible indicators of well-being. Yet, we suggest the provision of this detail has been at the expense of deployability. Indeed, MAP has not had a substantial impact on policy debate, despite Trewin and Hall (2005) suggesting otherwise. A search of Australian Parliamentary Hansard reveals MAP has been mentioned just three times in the House of Representatives and only once in the Senate since 1997. If elected representatives do not use MAP to promote, defend or challenge policies, MAP cannot be said to have successfully engaged the public in a discussion about how to measure progress. By way of comparison, the Hansard search reveals that the HDI has received 10 times as many mentions in parliamentary debates during the same period.

Statistics allow us to grasp and discuss complex phenomena spread across enormous populations. To do this, they invariably ignore important details. We can illustrate this by comparing MAP to HDI, since the latter enjoys greater usage in Australian and international debate. Saudi Arabia was ranked 34th on the HDI in 2014, above Croatia, Malta, Poland, Portugal and Slovakia. Yet, according to another plausible measure of national well-being – Freedom House's Freedom Index[2] – Saudi Arabia is one of only eight countries that currently attracts the 'Worst of the Worst' designation (others include North Korea and Syria) with the lowest possible scores on 'freedom', 'political rights' and 'civil liberties'. Should the ABS adopt HDI as a measure of progress, given its greater currency? The simplicity of HDI means it can be quickly invoked to support or oppose political arguments, but as a measure of well-being or progress it is also vulnerable to legitimate criticisms of incompleteness.

Headline statistics such as GDP and HDI are more likely to be used because they can be quickly deployed in news bulletins, parliamentary questions and doorstop interviews. They are conducive to attention-grabbing headlines. The MAP dashboard cannot be deployed in these ways. It generates detailed but contradictory findings, conveys relationships between dimensions of progress using imprecise narratives, and invariably presents an ambiguous answer to the question, 'is life in Australia getting better?' Thus measurers must make a choice: if they want their measures to be widely used, they must engage in simplification and exclusion in the process of definition and measurement. While the ABS aspires to move towards consensus on a new, easily deployable, single measure of progress over time through public dialogue, we argue this is unrealistic because it underestimates the cultural and political pluralism at the core of late-modern life.

Thirdly and finally, measurers must grapple with the dilemma of designing their indicators to be responsive to local measurement priorities while at the same time making those numbers consistent with measures used globally. This reflects a basic dilemma of statistics: the process of fitting people or things into standardised categories so that they can be counted as members of populations inevitably conceals some local idiosyncrasies (Latour 1993). For official statistics, a key question is at what level – local, national or global – is standardisation imposed? Historically, categories have been fixed at the national level, but increasingly they are being set globally, as countries move to adopt international classifications in the measurement of virtually all aspects of national life (Higgins and Larner 2010). A major advantage of global standardisation is that it allows comparisons of performance across multiple jurisdictions. In an age of cultural and economic globalisation this urge to compare is ubiquitous. HDI and other single-number indicators are arguably used more than MAP in part because they allow discussion of other nations. HDI and other global headline measures therefore drive and are driven by the imperative to rank and compare across borders. By starting with what Australians care about, MAP shuts off this crucial potential use. MAP thus faces a dilemma: should it approach the design of indicators organically using the priorities of Australians, or does it encourage wider use by adopting the external categories supplied by a global community of quantifiers?

These dilemmas highlight the difficult choices that confront measurers as they seek to create numerical indicators for formerly unquantified elements of government performance and social life. Future research could employ detailed qualitative analysis of the views and actions of measurers, to determine how they manage such dilemmas, and how their choices shape the impact of indicators on political discourse. Such research would advance our understanding of the power and limits of governmental quantification.

Notes

1. http://www.oecdbetterlifeindex.org/
2. freedomhouse.org/report/freedom-world/freedom-world-2015#.VcAhPOc1Cwl

Disclosure statement

No potential conflict of interest was reported by the authors.

References

ABS (Australian Bureau of Statistics). 2004a. "ABS Releases Measures of Australia's Progress." Accessed July 17, 2015. http://www.abs.gov.au/ausstats/abs@.nsf/mediareleasesbytopic/2BFA39220B7D32E1CA256E7C008253D4?OpenDocument.
ABS (Australian Bureau of Statistics). 2004b. *Measures of Australia's Progress 2004*. Canberra: Australian Bureau of Statistics.
ABS (Australian Bureau of Statistics). 2009. "Relationships Between Domains of Progress. Measures of Australia's Progress: Summary Indicators, 2008." Accessed July 30, 2015. http://www.abs.gov.au/ausstats/abs@.nsf/3d68c56307742d8fca257090002029cd/5fddd465aba670acca2574d30012f0f1!OpenDocument.
ABS (Australian Bureau of Statistics). 2010. *Trust in ABS and ABS Statistics: A Survey of Specialist Users and the General Community*. Canberra: Australian Bureau of Statistics.
ABS (Australian Bureau of Statistics). 2012. *Measures of Australia's Progress Aspirations for Our Nation: A Conversation with Australians about Progress*. Canberra: Australian Bureau of Statistics.
ABS (Australian Bureau of Statistics). 2013a. "Information Paper: Measures of Australia's Progress Proposed Statistical Indicators, 2013." Accessed July 10, 2015. http://www.abs.gov.au/ausstats/abs@.nsf/Lookup/1370.0.00.003main+features1122013.
ABS (Australian Bureau of Statistics). 2013b. "Is Australia progressing? The result are in." Commonwealth of Australia Accesses July 10, 2015, http://www.abs.gov.au/ausstats/abs@.nsf/Lookup/by%20Subject/1370.0~2013~Media%20Release~Is%20Australia%20progressing%3F%20The%20results%20are%20in%20(Media%20Release)%20~89.
ABS (Australian Bureau of Statistics). 2013c. *Measures of Australia's Progress 2013*. Canberra. Accessed July 10, 2015. http://www.abs.gov.au/ausstats/abs@.nsf/mf/1370.0
Arendt, H. 1973. *The Origins of Totalitarianism*. New York: Harcourt Brace Jovanovich.
Bagolin, I. 2004. *Human Development Index (HDI) – A Poor Representation to Human Development Approach*. Porto Alegre: University of Rio Grande do Sul, PUCRS.
Bates, W. 2009. "Gross National Happiness." *Asian-Pacific Economic Literature* 23 (2): 1–16.
Bauman, Z. 2000. *Liquid Modernity*. Cambridge: Polity Press.
Beck, U. 1992. *Risk Society: Towards a New Modernity*. London: Sage.
Beck, U. and E. Beck-Gernsheim. 2002. *Individualization: Institutionalized Individualism and Its Social and Political Consequences*. London: Sage.
Beck, U., A. Giddens, and S. Lash. 1994. *Reflexive Modernization: Politics, Tradition and Aesthetics in the Modern Social Order*. Stanford: Stanford University Press.
Bödeker, H. E. 2001. "On the Origins of the 'Statistical Gaze': Modes of Perception, Forms of Knowledge, and Ways of Writing in the Early Social Sciences." In *Little Tools of Knowledge: Historical Essays on Academic and Bureaucratic Practices*, edited by P. a. C. W. Becker, 169–195. Ann Arbor: University of Michigan Press.
Cobb, C., T. Halstead, and J. Rowe. 1995a. *The Genuine Progress Indicator*. San Francisco, CA: Redefining Progress.
Cobb, C., T. Halstead, and J. Rowe. 1995b. "If the GDP Is Up, Why Is America Down?" *Atlantic Monthly* 276: 59–79.

Costanza, R., M. Hart, J. Talberth, and S. Posner. 2009. "Beyond GDP: The Need for New Measures of Progress." *The Pardee Papers*, No. 4, Boston: Boston University.

Daly, H. E. 1996. *Beyond Growth: The Economics of Sustainable Development*. Boston:Beacon Press.

Daly, H. E., J. B. Cobb Jr, and C. W. Cobb. 1989. *For the Common Good: Redirecting the Economy Toward Community the Environment and a Sustainable Future*. Boston: Beacon Press.

Davidson, K., and L. Wilson. 2011. "Australia's Progress Undefined: A Critical Review of Measures of Australia's Progress (MAP)." *Australian Journal of Public Administration* 70 (1): 47–57. doi:10.1111/j.1467-8500.2011.00712.x.

Donaldson, P. 1992. *Economics of the Real World*. 3rd ed. London: Penguin.

Eckersley, R. 1998. "Shaping the Future to Human Needs." *Family Matters* 51 (Spring/Summer): 6–12.

Fellegi, I. P. 1996. "Characteristics of an Effective Statistical System." *Canadian Public Administration* 39 (1): 5–34.

Galbraith, J. K.. 1958. *The Affluent Society*. Boston: Houghton Mifflin Harcourt.

Giddens, A. 1991. *Modernity and Self-identity: Self and Society in the Late Modern Age*. Stanford: Stanford University Press.

Girvetz, H. 1963. *The Evolution of Liberalism*. New York: Collier Books.

Hajer, M. A. 2009. *Authoritative Governance: Policy Making in the Age of Mediatization*. Oxford: Oxford University Press.

Hall, P. A. 1993. "Policy Paradigms, Social Learning, and the State: The Case of Economic Policymaking in Britain." *Comparative Politics* 25 (3): 275–296.

Hibbing, J. R., and E. Theiss-Morse. 2002. *Stealth Democracy: Americans' Beliefs About How Government Should Work*. Cambridge: Cambridge University Press.

Higgins, V., and W. Larner. 2010. *Calculating the Social: Standards and the Reconfiguration of Governing*. Basingstoke: Palgrave Macmillan.

Inglehart, R. 1977. *The Silent Revolution: Changing Values and Political Styles Among Western Publics*. Princeton: Princeton University Press.

Jessop, B. 1999. "The Changing Governance of Welfare: Recent Trends in Its Primary Functions, Scale, and Modes of Coordination." *Social Policy & Administration* 33 (4): 348–359.

Latour, B. 1993. *We Have Never Been Modern*. Cambridge, MA: Harvard University Press.

Lawn, P. A. 2003. "A Theoretical Foundation to Support the Index of Sustainable Economic Welfare (ISEW), Genuine Progress Indicator (GPI), and Other Related Indexes." *Ecological Economics* 44 (1): 105–118.

Lawn, P. A. 2005. "An Assessment of the Valuation Methods Used to Calculate the Index of Sustainable Economic Welfare (ISEW), Genuine Progress Indicator (GPI), and Sustainable Net Benefit Index (SNBI)." *Environment, Development and Sustainability* 7 (2): 185–208.

Mannheim, K. 1936. *Ideology and Utopia: An Introduction to the Sociology of Knowledge*. New York: Harvest.

Marcuss, R. D., and R. E. Kane. 2007. "US National Income and Product Statistics." *Survey of Current Business* 87: 2–32.

Mayer-Schönberger, V., and K. Cukier. 2013. *Big Data: A Revolution That Will Transform How We Live, Work, and Think*. London: John Murray.

Miller, P., L. Kurunmaki, and T. O'Leary. 2010. "Calculating the Social: Standards and the Reconfiguration of Governing." In *Calculating Hybrids*, edited by Higgins, V., and W. Larner. Basingstoke: Palgrave Macmillan.

Nisbett, R. 1994. *History of the Idea of Progress*. New Brunswick: Transaction.

Saunders, P. 2002. "Whose Progress? A Response to the ABS Report Measures of Australia's Progress." *Issue Analysis* 25: 1–15.

Schepelmann, P., Y. Goossens, and A. Makipaa. 2009. *Towards Sustainable Development: Alternatives to GDP for Measuring Progress*. Wuppertal Spezial: Wuppertal Institut für Klima, Umwelt und Energie.

Schwartz, J. 2010. "Is GDP an Obsolete Measure of Progress?" *Time*, January 30. http://content.time.com/time/business/article/0,8599,1957746,00.html.

Shergold, P. 2011. "Measuring wellbeing is still in the too-hard basket." *The Sydney Morning Herald*, November 30.

Spadafora, D. 1990. *The Idea of Progress in Eighteenth-century*. Britain: Yale University Press.

Stiglitz, J. E., A. Sen, and J.-P. Fitoussi. 2010. Report by the Commission on the Measurement of Economic Performance and Social Progress. Paris: Commission on the Measurement of Economic Performance and Social Progress.

Sutton, T. M. 2011. "A Response to 'Australia's Progress Undefined: A Critical Review of Measures of Australia's Progress (MAP)'." *Australian Journal of Public Administration* 70 (3): 327–331. doi:10.1111/j.1467-8500.2011.00733.x.

Talberth, J., C. Cobb, and N. Slattery. 2007. *The Genuine Progress Indicator 2006*. Oakland, CA: Redefining Progress, 26.

Trewin, D. 2002. *Measuring Australia's Progress*. Canberra: Australian Bureau of Statistics.

Trewin, D. 2004. *Measures of Australia's Progress 2004*. Canberra: Australian Bureau of Statistics.

Trewin, D. 2006. *Measures of Australia's Progress*. Canberra: Australian Bureau of Statistics.

Trewin, D., and J. Hall, 2005. "Measures of Australia's Progress-A Case Study of a National Report Based on Key Economic, Social and Environment Indicators." In *Statistics, Knowledge and Policy: Key Indicators to Inform Decision-making*, edited by OECD, 88–103. Paris: OECD.

UNSD. 2003. *The Handbook of Statistical Organization, Third Edition: The Operation and Organization of a Statistical Agency*. New York: United Nations Statistics Division.

NAPLAN data: a new policy assemblage and mode of governance in Australian schooling

Alison Gable and Bob Lingard

ABSTRACT

As part of a policy assemblage, the National Assessment Program – Literacy and Numeracy (NAPLAN) is representative of a new mode of governance for Australia's schooling systems, indicative of international trends in educational accountability based on testing. The policy assumption was that the introduction of a national performance measurement system would tightly couple school practices to national agendas targeted at improving learning outcomes. This paper presents a comparative case study of two primary schools within a single Queensland region to interrogate how coupling and decoupling strategies are enacted in respect of the policy usage of NAPLAN data. The granular analysis of the governance relationship between the school principals and their supervisors is set against the politics, policies and pressures of NAPLAN that recast the initiative as high stakes for systems, schools and their leadership. Specifically, we argue that Queensland's choice and enactment of policy instruments have produced a new mode of governance of principal conduct, but one mediated by the specific contexts of the two schools. The analysis shows how this mode has precipitated two types of decoupling.

1. Introduction

National testing was introduced in Australian schooling in 2008, following the election of the Rudd federal Labor government in 2007. This is NAPLAN – the National Assessment Program – Literacy and Numeracy administered to all students in Years 3, 5, 7 and 9 in all schools in May each year. Whilst NAPLAN itself is not a traditional high stakes test – there is little riding on its outcomes for students – we would argue that the politics, policies and pressures surrounding it, documented later in the paper, have ensured that it has become high stakes for systems, schools and teachers with flow on effects to students (Howell 2016), curriculum and pedagogy (Nichols and Berliner 2007). It is thus the surrounding policies – we might see NAPLAN as a component part of a broader policy assemblage[1] – that make NAPLAN high stakes.

In terms of this policy assemblage, we are referring *inter alia* to the federal government funded website, *My School*, an important policy artefact, introduced in 2010, which makes publicly available the comparative performance of all schools on NAPLAN. The website reports average school results in all domains and year levels and compares these with national averages and with the performance of 60 statistically similar schools in terms of their student populations. We are also referring to the usage of such data for accountability purposes in relation to some national policies and at state level as well. There are two official aims of NAPLAN: 'to help drive improvements in student outcomes and provide increased accountability for the community' (ACARA 2011), ¶4. In Queensland, for example, given the political panic evoked by the state's comparatively poor performance on the first test in 2008, NAPLAN has become a focus of policy and of the accountability regime. At the Queensland level and nationally (in a range of so-called National Partnership during the federal Labor period, 2007–2013), targeted improvements on NAPLAN have been important drivers of schooling policy and practice.

There is a plethora of critical literature specifically about NAPLAN in educational research (Comber and Nixon 2009; Klenowski and Wyatt-Smith 2012; Lingard, Thompson, and Sellar 2016). As a point of distinction from that growing body of research literature in education, this paper draws upon the political sociology of Lascoumes and Le Galès (2007) to consider NAPLAN as central to educational accountability. This is what Lascoumes and Le Gales call *audience democracy*, a particular constitution of transparency as manifested in the *My School* website.

Additionally, we draw on Bromley and Powell's (2012) two-level typology of decoupling practices within organisations to identify the extent of changes related to, and professional impact of, NAPLAN. Our focus is on a granular analysis of a new mode of governance of principal conduct as a consequence of the policy instrument choices.

The paper's intention is to provide focused analysis of the working relationship of two principals of two primary schools (situated in vastly different socio-economic communities) with their departmental supervisors, undertaken during case studies of schools from one Queensland Department of Education region. We apply the theoretical resources mentioned above to understand the course of policy instrument choice (e.g. from *My School* to the use of 'like school' measures) and its impact on the role of principals.

Thus, the paper is in one sense conceptual in approach. However, the empirical cases are also used as to illustrate the utility of these theoretical resources.

This paper considers the organisational pressures on these school case sites as a consequence of the combination of two *new* policy instruments offering an alternative to traditional command and control modes of governance (Lascoumes and Le Galès 2007). We argue that the use of *information-* and *communication-*based tools, such as NAPLAN reporting (and the My School website) in combination with *de facto* and *de jure* standards, such as NAPLAN performance indicators and targets, serve as powerful contexts for decoupling practices.

We first outline the policy setting of NAPLAN, nationally and in Queensland, then move to elaborate the theoretical and methodological framings of the research, before presenting our case studies. Put succinctly, whereas NAPLAN was instigated to improve student learning, the effect on practice has been to focus on improving tests scores and thus decoupling professional practice from the broader goals of schooling as articulated in Australia in the *Melbourne Declaration of Goals for Australia's Schools* (MCEETYA 2008). Yet, as we will also demonstrate, the specific contexts of the two schools mediated this impact and the enactment of NAPLAN framed accountabilities (cf Ball, Maguire, and Braun 2012). We conclude with a discussion of insights from the research.

The policy setting and the constitution of NAPLAN as high stakes in Queensland

As noted above, in 2007 a national Labor government was elected in Australia that had campaigned *inter alia* on a platform of introducing a national curriculum for schools, national literacy and numeracy testing for all schools (census testing) and a renewed focus on equity, using comparative performance data for policy interventions.

Subsequently a new statutory authority, the Australian Curriculum, Assessment and Reporting Authority (ACARA), was established to oversee the implementation of this reform agenda, focusing on the development of the national curriculum for the years from pre-school to year 10 and introducing and managing NAPLAN. Whilst the first NAPLAN tests were conducted in 2008 the results were made publicly available from 2010 after the creation by ACARA of the *My School* website. *My School* makes public the performance on NAPLAN of all schools at all year levels and for the four dimensions of the test, namely, reading, writing, language conventions (literacy) and numeracy. The comparative data for each school on *My School* are set against national averages, against benchmarks and against the performance of statistically similar schools as measured by an Index of Socio-Educational Advantage (ICSEA).

Such data have become central to the now dominant approach to school accountability across the nation and internationally. Under the federal Labor governments (2007–2013), a series of National Partnerships on schooling used such performance data to target and fund schools, but also for accountability purposes. There was also accompanying performance bonuses for school principals if targets set for NAPLAN improvement were achieved for National Partnership schools. The election of the Conservative Abbott government in 2013 saw the end of the National Partnerships and associated redistributive approach to school funding. However, the policy usage of NAPLAN data, the focus of politicians, the public availability of comparative data on *My School*, associated with extensive media coverage (Mockler 2016), ensured that NAPLAN remained high stakes with real effects.

NAPLAN became even more high stakes in Queensland after the state's apparent comparative poor performance in 2008. In response and in a context of much critical media coverage and political panic, the then Premier Anna Bligh established a review of Queensland's performance chaired by Professor Geoff Masters, CEO of the Australian Council for Educational Research. This review made a number of recommendations, including ensuring that Queensland students were test literate and well prepared to sit NAPLAN. The main outcome though was the creation of an annual Teaching and Learning Audit of every school as a concerted system-wide approach for improvement on NAPLAN (abolished after the election of the Conservative Newman government in late 2013). A longer term outcome of the Review was the moving of Year 7 into secondary schooling in 2015, as the Premier believed the different structure of schooling in both Victoria and New South Wales (Year 7 in secondary schools) was a factor in their superior NAPLAN performance (and also in their better performance on the international Trends in Maths and Science Study) (see Lingard and Sellar 2013).

Another important example of a structural effect of NAPLAN on the Department of Education in Queensland was the creation in 2010 of Assistant Regional Director – School Performance (ARD-SP) positions in each of the regional administrative areas of the system (Bloxham, Ehrich, and Iyer 2015) and linked to a senior performance management position at head office. The supervisory and development roles of ARD-SP positions were putatively established to build principal capacity in delivering improved school performance. These positions remain in place across changes of government. Along with ongoing media coverage, all of these developments strengthened the construction of NAPLAN as a high stakes test in Queensland with system, school, principal and teacher accountability restructured around performance data sets with NAPLAN being central.

These pressure constituting NAPLAN as high stakes did not ease under the conservative Newman state government (2013–2015). On receipt of federal government monies following the 2013 election of the Abbott government, the state put in place the *Great Teachers = Great Results* programme, whereby each school had to explain how the extra funding would be used to achieve targeted improvements on NAPLAN. The Palaszczuk Labor government, elected in Queensland in 2015 has abolished this policy, which sought to place all school leaders on performance contracts linked to improvement on performance data. The Newman government also introduced a new mode of devolution with its Independent Public Schools programme. This policy also utilised NAPLAN and other performance data as its central mode of accountability. Indeed, we might argue following Lawn's analysis of similar policy developments in England, that data have become central to department/school and ARD-SP/principal relationships and indeed to the construction of the 'system' – a 'systemless system' (Lawn 2013).

This documenting of the encompassing policy setting in which the NAPLAN policy tool is situated confirms the ways in which NAPLAN has become high stakes with real organisational and professional impacts. This is the policy/contextual backdrop to the case studies of two schools, which constitute the empirical focus of the paper. What we are seeing here is a vernacular or path dependent expression of what Sahlberg (2011) has called the Global Education Reform Movement, an Anglo-American reform agenda, focusing on test-based modes of accountability, reductive curriculum stress on literacy and numeracy, and competition between schools around a data- and performance-based quasi-market in schooling. The research interviews were conducted in 2013, as were other data on the two schools, two years post the introduction of the ARDs.

Theory and methodology

Australia's schooling reform efforts have presumed NAPLAN would facilitate tighter coupling of local school practices to national and state-level school improvement agendas. Accordingly, this paper utilises Bromley and Powell's (2012) typologies of decoupling practices to identify the extent of organisational change contingent on policy instrument choices (Lascoumes and Le Galès 2007). Specifically, we consider the impact of these *choices* for the governance of principal conduct in two Queensland primary schools to demonstrate how and in what circumstances, NAPLAN's policy instrumentation can generate heterogeneous responses.

Bromley and Powell's (2012) view that decoupling practices are a consequence of context, rather than cynical management strategies, focuses attention on external (e.g. public and community) and organisational pressures (e.g. policy and politics), when navigating policy practices and core professional activity. They argue that despite seemingly compliant behaviour, an organisation may not achieve a policy's objective as a consequence of opaque and attenuated links between activity and outcome. This *means-end* form of decoupling provides an important alternative to *policy-practice* decoupling and a comparative opportunity for isolating the chain reactions of the policy context. Means-end decoupling refers to *symbolic implementation* (Bromley and Powell 2012) of the policy, when changes to organisational routines have little or no relation to intended outcomes. Policy-practice decoupling refers to *symbolic adoption* (Bromley and Powell 2012) of the policy that is ceremonial like, disconnected from day-to-day practices.

These approaches to understanding de-coupling in policy to practise relationships are complementary to other approaches to slippages accompanying policy implementation. A common view has been to see such slippages resulting from professional, situated mediation of policy intentions (McLaughlin 2006). This can be understood either as policy infidelity in practice or viewed more positively as context-specific professional knowledge mediating universalist policy intentions. A second way to think about the policy to practise relationship is to talk of 'policy enactment' (see Ball, Maguire, and Braun 2012). This approach sees school context (referring both to the external and internal contexts of a given school) and professional agentive mediations of policy into practice as central factors in how any given policy is enacted in schools. As a point of distinction, our focus is on how the choice of policy instrument instantiates a new mode of governance of principal practices. In the analysis, though, we acknowledge the specific school contextual mediation of such a mode of governance. In our case, this is acknowledgement of the mediating effects of different socio-economic contexts of the schools on principal practices in relation to NAPLAN.

Information- and *communication-based* policy instruments articulate *audience democracy* so that a moral obligation to publicly inform or disclose renews and reinforces the answerability of professionals (Lascoumes and Le Galès 2007). From an organisational perspective, such accountability of states, systems, schools, principals and teachers for NAPLAN outcomes serves to fragment the environment (Bromley and Powell 2012), requiring schools to navigate an increasingly uncoordinated body of stakeholders holding multiple and conflicting organisational expectations. School responses to these external pressures provide insights into the audiences governing professional activity.

De jure and *de facto* standards neutralise the political intentions behind their implementation as a consequence of their promoted and apparent objectivity and in so doing depoliticise them. Standards and benchmarks are typically negotiated, developed and cooperatively executed (Lascoumes and Le Galès 2007) to establish a set of internal relations, for example, between an education department and teachers. *De jure* standards are targeted at informing the focused design of new 'products' (Borraz 2007), in this case literacy and numeracy practices. However, as standards can be imposed or utilised as a choice mechanism (Lascoumes and Le Galès 2007), they also have the potential to shape external relations, for example, between schools and parents. Here, NAPLAN performance becomes the *de facto* standard for judging a student or a school's performance. This dual dynamic is argued to shift 'rulemaking from the state to civil society' (Borraz 2007, 58), so that decision making about implementation of standards is left to 'interested parties, without political intervention' (2007, 58). This is the new mode of governance.

In organisational terms, the use of standards rationalises the working environment to produce coherent activity with predictable outcomes. These external criteria may have little to do with a school's core goals or the broader goals of schooling systems, but nevertheless shape its organisational structure as a consequence of its navigations of pressures to conform to authority or public judgements (Bromley and Powell 2012). When and why schools implement activities that are weakly linked to goals (means-end decoupling) or resist activities to protect core goals (policy-practice decoupling) provides some insight into the capacity of benchmarks and targets to bring a predictability to professional activity.

In view of the correlation between student socio-economic status and performance, including on NAPLAN, the case study schools were selected from pools of possible case sites based on student enrolments, staff numbers, student characteristics and either high or low ICSEA scores. Woodlands State School (WSS) services a socio-educationally advantaged community with a stable, homogenous student body, many of whom are destined for enrolment in non-government secondary schools. Edgefield State School (ESS) is located in a disadvantaged, low socio-economic area with students reflecting a wide spread of minority communities.[2]

The cases reported in this paper are part of a larger Australian Research Council funded research project on performance measurement (PM) across the public sector with a focus on schooling, higher education, and health policy. The project has been concerned to document, understand and theorise the impacts of PM as a new mode of governance. The empirical databases include policy analysis of relevant documents and a range of interviews across the public sector at various levels of the structure, including interviews with what we might see as the street-level bureaucrats/professionals, who implement or enact, and are affected by, new modes of performance governance.

In this paper, we utilise interviews with two ARDs-SP and two school principals.

Where pertinent we quote directly from those interviews. Also interviewed were 9 teachers and 3 other administrators across the two schools, but we do not quote directly from these. Analysis of the thematically coded data involved processes of data reduction and data display (Miles and Huberman 1994), assisted by NVIVO to facilitate conclusion drawing, concept building and confirmation.

The cases: Woodlands and Edgefield state schools

Structural change

As noted earlier, the introduction of ARDs-SP initiated a new systemic professional relationship for principals. Here we see a specific organisational response to the policy tool, NAPLAN and the significance of test performance to the structuring of systems and accountability. One ARD-SP reflected on the impact of this new relationship:

> If I look back at 2011, there wasn't an urgency around the national testing. Schools pretty much were cruising along, and principals hadn't given a great deal of attention to the national testing and their overall school performance, and probably weren't that interested. But with the appointments of the [ARDs] ... we've probably refocused schools on what their business was, and how they could influence an improvement in student learning outcomes.

We see in this observation an emphasis on improving student learning outcomes, which becomes reduced in practice, as we will show, to improvement on NAPLAN tests.

At the time of data collection, a 10-page, A3 sized document of school data called the School Performance Profile formed the basis of biannual reviews between the ARDs-SP and principals. The profile provided a rich source of expanded measures of performance to include enrolment, attendance, retention and progression rates, NAPLAN results, other assessment data, workforce and financial data, as well as achievement and improvement measures against targets such as NAPLAN performance indicators. The document was made possible via the Department's centralised, web-based information management system, *OneSchool* (DETE 2013, 2), effectively liberating data from the confines of classrooms and principals' offices. In relation to such matters, Lawn suggests that this allows 'the centre to shape, direct and steer a system that only it fully determines and views as a single, complex system' (2013, 232).

The biannual review process encapsulates the organisational impact of policy instrumentation (Lascoumes and Le Galès 2007), combining *information* (expanded measures of student performance) and *communication* (school profiles) with *de jure* and *de facto* standards (national benchmarks, including 'like school' measures, state and local targets) to reshape the social relations of teaching in Queensland public schooling. The change in attitudes to NAPLAN referred to above by the ARD-SP suggests a shift in power relations as a consequence of how data, reporting and benchmarking were re-constructed and re-operationalised through the biannual reviews with impacts on the governance of principals' work.

The organisational/socio-political context of NAPLAN

Education Queensland firmly established an institutional rhetoric linking teaching and learning activities to expected improvements in student learning. One interviewee stated that:

> the bonus came when [the Director-General] said to 1300 people, 'This is what I want you to do, and I want you to all do that now, and I just want you to focus on teaching and learning' … now, no matter where a teacher goes, they'll hear the same message and experience the same accountability. (ARD 2)

Thus, the management of teaching and learning was institutionally positioned as the preferred *means* to achieve the *ends* of improved NAPLAN performance and a causal connection between professional activity and NAPLAN outcomes was posited by the Department's executive (Bromley and Powell 2012). The latter was an elision of the broader intended focus on improving student learning, which was now synonymous with improved NAPLAN performance. These rationales are consequential for understanding the Department's internal organisational restructuring through data and their effects.

In the aftermath of the political panic documented earlier, it became apparent schools were not *value-adding* to student background, producing a system narrative of under-performing schools in affluent suburbs. After 2010, publicly available data on NAPLAN demonstrated this quite clearly with the 'like school' measures. Schools situated in populations with significant socio-educational advantages are often referred to as green and leafy, reflecting their physical surrounds and advantages stemming from communities with strong social, economic and cultural capital. As a consequence of perceived stable and privileged school and teaching environments, professional activity in these green and leafy schools was constructed as the *cause* of student under-achievement when compared with performance against 'like schools' nation-wide. It is significant that the interviews with the ARDs-SP extended this view, in relation to middle-class schools, to encompass a stance that *all* schools could make a difference in student performance irrespective of their socio-economic context. However, discursively the ARDs' arguments were always about the poor performance of middle-class schools in Brisbane compared with those in Sydney and Melbourne. The post-2008 focus subsequently moved to the cohort of students *most* able to meet national benchmarks for literacy and numeracy.

> If we went back to the data in our region in 2008, '09 and '10, even our leafy greens were doing really poorly on NAPLAN. Probably some of our highest performers were the lower ICSEA schools. So, we could show you that, in '08 and '09 and '10 that our leafy green schools weren't doing so well, ... But now, that's changed ... and certainly the kids in the leafy green schools should be performing. (ARD1)

Underpinning this transformation was a commitment to managerial accountability, 'rigorously prosecuted through the use of corporate data ... as the basis for ARDs-SP to determine school and principal achievement and improvement' (Bloxham, Ehrich, and Iyer 2015, 361).

The interviewed ARDs-SP provided rich descriptions of the biannual performance reviews with principals. Collegiate conversations were directed at professional reflection on data, processes and outcomes. Negotiated targets set with the principals in the first meeting were revisited at the end of the year and explanation sought as to the relative success of professional activity in relation to the targets.

Significantly, the conversation on student gain focused on a single table in the document (drawn from *My School*), indicating the school's relative performance against the statistically similar schools across Australia. This comparison against 'like schools' served as stimulus to further discussion about improvement to spotlight potential professional complacency. One ARD presented the comparative results of a green and leafy school to describe the subsequent conversation:

> ... that's an example of a high ICSEA school – its data is always above the national mean, which is good, fantastic. But 'how are you going against your similar schools?', and that would be the conversation for that school. 'Well, you're not doing so well against your similar schools'. The principals say, 'yes, but we're doing as well as we can, or we can't do any better'. 'But there must be schools in Sydney that are doing that little bit better'. (ARD1)

Accordingly, the comparative table of 'like schools' was used to disrupt the suggestion that postcode was a greater influence on NAPLAN performance than professional activity – school leadership and teaching practices. This narrative also extended to low ICSEA schools, supported by a rationale that teachers carried low expectations of their students. One interviewee responding to the question of student-background commented: 'Yes, yes. That's a rationale that is usually tabled by principals in low-performing schools as an excuse why they were where they're at' (ARD2). We note again though in all examples of improvement articulated by the ARDs of NAPLAN it was schools in higher socio-economic areas that were referred to. We can see at work here the focus on quality teaching as the decontextualised 'cause' of student learning rearticulated as improved scores on NAPLAN.

In addition, the ARDs had clear expectations as to how principals would liberate the data for performance governance involving an enculturation of data usage to diagnose, inform and to develop consistent practices, combined with collegiate mentoring and capacity building. One ARD commented that:

> If principals don't make that a focus, they're not going to have quality teaching and they're not going to have quality learning outcomes. ... the principals would be taking a huge risk not to have some sort of mentoring feedback program within the school. (ARD1)

The region had clear managerial expectations of its principals and their use of data to drive professional activity and therefore student performance. This was constructed as a process of clarifying and rationalising priorities and enculturating teaching staff in similar use of data to achieve accountability for student improvement.

Local leadership and increased accountabilities

As NAPLAN testing cannot be circumvented, meeting, resisting or moderating external pressures for accountability rest firmly with a school's leadership. In light of vastly different contexts, it is unsurprising the two principals adopted alternative approaches to performance governance. The different organisational processes deployed in response to NAPLAN and the biannual reviews closely align to Bromley and Powell's (2012) contemporary typologies of decoupling practices. The extent to which these accountability demands support or conflict with what is deemed by the principals as core professional activity, may explain why data usage becomes implemented (means-end decoupling), or merely symbolic (policy-practice decoupling). Furthermore, the two cases show the significance of contextual mediation in the impact of policy in schools (Ball, Maguire, and Braun 2012).

The data strategy deployed by the Principal of WSS, tightly coupled to the model proposed by the ARDs, focused on information gathering, action and professional assessment. Six-week cycles of data conversations between senior managers and year-level teachers, in combination with collegiate evaluation of individual teacher performance, were implemented. The conversations concentrated on the use of internal assessment data, teacher observations, student tracking, regional targets, year-level planning and analysis of teaching practices. Typical of means-end decoupling, the school's emphasis on measurement to inform practice appeared to be 'a valued activity in itself' (Bromley and Powell 2012, 24). We note also how the introduction of NAPLAN has increased the amount of formal testing conducted by schools using other available tests of literacy and numeracy. In addition, there was pressure from the WSS parent community after the release of the first NAPLAN performance data for the school to achieve better results. This abated once improvements in this performance were achieved – audience accountability at work.

It was evident from the teaching staff that these substantial organisational routines were viewed as an opportunity for professional dialogue and development (see Henman and Gable 2015). The principal's leadership was highly valued and recognised as supporting a welcomed level of professionalism and professional dialogue. It was apparent that staff accountability for student improvement had rapidly become engrained at WSS as normative practice within the school, described in the following comment:

> the teachers know – and that's when we have those data chats. We talk about this. I should be able to go into any classroom and say 'Who's your best performer in reading?' ... and they

should be able to tell me who's their lower performer but most importantly, they need to be able to [answer] 'What are you going to do to make it better?'. (WSS principal)

The organisational complexity evident at WSS reflects a response to an increasingly fragmented systemic environment, the 'systemless system' we referred to earlier. The high visibility of the school's NAPLAN performance in the local media created substantial (both real and imagined) parental expectations of good and improved student outcomes. Indeed, initially there was some parental pressure upon the school in terms of the collective NAPLAN performance. More significantly, Education Queensland's narrative of under-performing green and leafy, middle-class schools, in combination with the introduction of biannual performance reviews, appear to have magnified institutional pressures. In this instance, the means to achieving ongoing improvements in student NAPLAN performance, and therefore legitimacy, was via adoption of data practices deemed appropriate by Education Queensland.

ESS's dynamic and heterogeneous community of immigrant, refugee and disadvantaged, low socio-economic populations provided complex and challenging teaching and learning contexts. Staff considered NAPLAN testing privileged the type of students who *did not* attend the school (see Henman and Gable 2015). The principal viewed NAPLAN data as contributing little to shape professional activity beyond targets for improvement. In addition, the school profile data were regarded as limited in their capacity to reflect the school's teaching and learning challenges. This distrust in the data served as an important rationale for the principal:

> Some of the comparisons that are in there are not particularly useful. .... In terms of the minute pieces of data that are in there, I think somebody who is a data fiend would find them fascinating, and some of them have a purpose. But you can't drill teachers in every minute piece of data when their focus is on whether the child can read the word that they've been trying to teach them for three weeks. There is a very different focus ... .in terms of some of that big picture thinking, we don't go into minute detail, because that's not what is relevant for the classroom teacher. (ESS Principal)

Accordingly, performance data were almost quarantined to the senior administrative team at ESS. Whilst day-to-day classroom- and school-based assessment practices reflected those of WSS, use of these data was left to the professional judgement of classroom teachers and their year-level teams. Teachers were encouraged to take ownership of their classroom planning, and performance evaluation related to annual appraisals. The school's leadership effectively served as a data buffer to protect core teaching activities; building students' social, emotional and cultural capacity to participate in learning.

The principal's resistance to Departmental pressures to implement data routines, is indicative of policy-practice decoupling as a protective response (Bromley and Powell 2012). The principal's unwillingness to use national and school-based assessment data for performance management inside the school suggests a conflict between accountability pressures and professional identity, reflective of a professional reading of the school's context and the needs of students. It is important to note this did not mean an abrogation of responsibility for student learning. Indeed, the teachers expressed a view that there were more important and pressing matters to focus on than pushing up NAPLAN scores. The protection of staff from managerialist and accountability agendas allowed a focus on more relevant, yet unmeasurable aspects of teaching and learning and professional care. This counter-conduct by the principal (Niesche 2013) subsequently serving as an internal mode of professional accountability to students.

Local leadership, targets and standards

In Queensland public schools, the biannual performance reviews included discussions on NAPLAN performance measures and local improvement plans in negotiating school targets to set the performance governance context.

> They all have targets. They also have targets around national minimum standards – how many kids they're going to get to the national minimum standard. But the more important one is the upper two bands, because the upper two bands will impact on the mean ... That's their goal for the year, and then they can report back on that. It's the conversation around if we achieved it or didn't achieve it that's really powerful. (ARD1)

WSS had an enviable position with most students performing substantially above the national average. The core challenge for the principal, cognisant of the students' capabilities, was to 'magnify their abilities to continue and grow' (WSS Principal). External pressure to maintain focus on already high performing students in an effort to increase the percentage reaching the top two bands was further compounded by the need to demonstrate improvements against similar schools, evident in the following comment:

> Originally, as a principal, I didn't care about 'like schools' but when I received those two marks that clearly indicated we weren't good enough, I said to the staff – and we've responded accordingly. (WSS Principal)

However, it was acknowledged by the staff of WSS that students came to them 'learning ready' and that their teaching practices might not produce similar outcomes in disadvantaged areas, thereby voicing an uncomfortable causal indeterminacy between teaching activity and outcomes. The principal made reference to their 'luck' in having very capable students able to meet NAPLAN targets by virtue of the school's socio-economic location. The continued engagement with data routines is suggestive of means-end decoupling, where professional activity is arguably linked to 'operational systems such as accounting, personnel management, evaluation, or monitoring' (Bromley and Powell 2012, 496), rather than student outcomes. Nevertheless, the impact of this was a standardisation of practices across the school and the enculturation of auditable professional activity, despite uncertainties about achieving NAPLAN improvement.

Students of ESS performed substantially below the national average in NAPLAN. The challenges for the principal extended beyond the problems of literacy and numeracy to issues associated with the impact of cultural barriers, poverty and trauma on learning.

> To be honest, for some of the families, I'm really excited when I see some of those kids in school the next day, because my worry when they went home was that they wouldn't make it the next day, ... as a school we have really high ownership of the people in our community, and we want them to have opportunities. (ESS Principal)

A further challenge for the principal rested with navigating institutional demands and expectations. In this respect, the narrative that student background would not be taken into consideration appeared to overwhelm the potential for improvement. This frustration was evident when the principal remarked:

> I'm not sure that some of the people making decisions have any idea about the complexities of some of the lives of our children. I think they would be shocked if they knew some of the circumstances under which our children live and work. (ESS Principal)

In light of student background, the institutional rhetoric linking teaching and learning activities to improvement in NAPLAN targets was meaningless. The targets set for the school were viewed as ambitious, unrealistic and symbolic. In the first instance a uniform state-wide target of performance on NAPLAN was set for each and every school in the state; such a uniform target denies contextual differences. Professional disempowerment was evident in the following comment:

> They were mandated by the state government at the start of the process, ... Now, it was never going to be a reality, and I understand that you have to have aspirational targets, but I think that was very hard for our staff. At an individual level, if you look at our student progress, you see significant changes. But when you put that together as a whole and you aggregate it against the state, you see that we're still in the red, and that's what people look at. (ESS Principal)

The weak, internal reinforcement and usage of performance data appeared a reaction to the poor fit between organisational and professional goals and professional capacity (Bromley and Powell 2012) to effect change, given the context in which the school was situated. As single state-wide improvement targets were considered unreachable, the rationalisation of professional activity hoped for by the performance reviews, was not realised.

Discussion and conclusion

Above we have documented something of the emergent relationship between a new organisational position – the ARDs-SP – and school principals, especially in relation to *de jure* and *de facto* standards (including national benchmarks, 'like schools' and system and local targets for improvement) and *information-* and *communication-based* (expanded measures in school profiles) policy instruments. These are set against Queensland's 2008 alarm over comparative NAPLAN performance, which recast policy priorities as state-wide improvement in school leadership practices and teacher pedagogies, both framed by expected productive usage of data. Here the work of both principals and teachers was repositioned as the major factor in and causes of school underperformance on NAPLAN. More specifically, the system embraced the notion of value-adding, but largely in relation to those students potentially most likely to improve state performance in meeting performance benchmarks. This discourse focused very specifically on the underperformance on 'like school' comparisons of middle-class schools in the green and leafy suburbs;[3] in our research, WSS. Whilst this narrative was very evident in the ARD interviews, we note the absence of examples in their interviews of discussion around the impact of low socio-economic contexts on school performance, such as with ESS. We would also suggest that one effect of 'like school' measures is that in putatively accounting for school context, such measures of themselves responsibilise school principals and teachers alone for school performance (Lingard, Sellar, and Savage 2014).

Our analysis suggests that the chain reaction resulting from these dynamics has produced two different modes of decoupling practices. In relation to WSS, we see decoupling as driven by institutional pressures rather than NAPLAN outcomes, suggestive of a managerial audience governing performance; here the ARD/principal relationship. As noted above, there was also in the first instance some parental pressure on WSS in relation to NAPLAN performance: parental audience affecting performance. Here the principal and the school sought legitimacy from both the system and the community. In respect of ESS, we see a decoupling driven by professional conflict and weak capacity to meet the system's policies of improvement on NAPLAN. We also see the denial by the system of recognising the support necessary for the school to achieve improvement targets. In this respect, the relationship between the ARD and principal is more ceremonial, as institutional pressures were resisted in favour of internal modes of professional regulation. The principal and teachers at ESS were adamant that NAPLAN data, including 'like school' comparisons, did not adequately capture and value the work the school was doing; indeed, there was no metric to do so. The principal saw, in our words, professional responsibility as building social, emotional and cultural capital amongst students, within the school and broader community. In a somewhat circular fashion, in both cases improved student learning has become synonymous with improved NAPLAN scores, whereas NAPLAN putatively was introduced as a way of improving learning.

How NAPLAN data are enacted rests heavily on the local mediation of the politics, policies and pressures described throughout the paper. The newest iteration of Queensland's performance regime, the *School Performance Assessment Framework*, suggests a strengthening of the mode of principal governance we have detailed. We would argue that this is not without risk. Organisationally, the type of means-end decoupling apparent in WSS's use of data achieves accountability objectives, but at the risk unwittingly of data usage becoming a valued activity in and of itself. We also anticipate that school leadership, of the type evident at ESS may be viewed as 'a moral and operational failure' of the system (Bromley and Powell 2012, 498) in its elision of consideration of socio-economic inequality. At risk, from this mode of governance, is principals' capacity to respond to the complex professional contexts in which teaching and learning of literacy and numeracy occur.

Acknowledgements

The authors would like to thank the schools and staff of Education Queensland for their generous participation in this research. In addition, we have greatly valued the thoughts and comments on this paper of our co-researchers Michele Foster and Paul Henman and two anonymous reviewers.

Disclosure statement

No potential conflict of interest was reported by the authors.

Funding

The research for this paper was supported under Australian Research Council's Discovery Projects funding scheme [DP110100803].

Notes

1. NAPLAN is one part of a composite set of policies – what we might see as an assemblage. Parts of this assemblage include the My School website, the Australian curriculum, various

accountability policies and various state government initiatives in education. On assemblage, see Deleuze and Guattari (1987).
2. Both school names are pseudonyms.
3. While like school measures responsibilise schools, principals and teachers in holding SES contexts constant, thus ensuring explanations of student performance are school and classroom based, in the interview with the ARD, examples of schools being able to make a difference referred only to middle class schools; perhaps a silent acknowledgment of the difficulties facing schools in low SES communities.

References

ACARA. 2011. "Why NAP." Australian Curriculum and Reporting Authority. Accessed July 20, 2015. http://www.nap.edu.au/about/why-nap.html.
Ball, Stephen J., Meg Maguire, and Annette Braun. 2012. *How Schools Do Policy*. London: Routledge.
Bloxham, Ray, Lisa Ehrich, and Radha Iyer. 2015. "Leading or Managing? Assistant Regional Directors, School Performance, in Queensland." *Journal of Educational Administration* 53 (2): 354–373.
Borraz, Olivier. 2007. "Governing Standards: The Rise of Standardization Processes in France and in the EU." *Governance: An International Journal of Policy, Administration, and Institutions* 20 (1): 57–84.
Bromley, Patricia, and Walter Powell. 2012. "From Smoke and Mirrors to Walking the Talk: Decoupling in the Contemporary World." *The Academy of Management Annals* 6 (1): 483–530.
Comber, Barbara, and Helen Nixon. 2009. "Teachers' Work and Pedagogy in an Era of Accountability." *Discourse: Studies in the Cultural Politics of Education* 30 (3): 333–345.
DETE. 2013. *OneSchool Evaluation 2013*. Brisbane: Department of Education, Training and Employment.
Deleuze, Gilles, and Félix Guattari. 1987. *A Thousand Plateaus*. Minneapolis, MN: University of Minnesota Press.
Henman, Paul, and Alison Gable. 2015. ""Schooling" Performance Measurement: The Politics of Governing Teacher Conduct in Australia." *Policy & Society* 34 (1): 63–74.
Howell, Angelique. 2016. "Exploring Children's Lived Experience of NAPLAN." In *National Testing in Schools*, edited by Bob Lingard, Greg Thompson, and Sam Sellar, 164–180. London: Routledge.
Klenowski, Val, and Claire Wyatt-Smith. 2012. "The Impact of High Stakes Testing: The Australian Story." *Assessment in Education: Principles, Policy & Practice* 19 (1): 65–79.
Lascoumes, Pierre, and Patrick Le Galès. 2007. "Introduction: Understanding Public Policy Through Its Instruments—From the Nature of Instruments to the Sociology of Public Policy Instrumentation." *Governance: An International Journal of Policy, Administration, and Institutions* 20 (1): 1–21.
Lawn, Martin. 2013. "A Systemless System." *European Educational Research Journal* 12 (2): 231–241.

Lingard, Bob, and Sam Sellar. 2013. "'Catalyst Data': Perverse Systemic Effects of Audit and Accountability in Australian Schooling." *Journal of Education Policy* 28 (5): 634–656.

Lingard, Bob, Sam Sellar, and Glenn Savage. 2014. "Re-articulating Social Justice as Equity in Schooling Policy: The Effects of Testing and Data Infrastructures." *British Journal of Sociology of Education* 35 (5): 710–730.

Lingard, Bob, Greg Thompson, and Sam Sellar, eds. 2016. *National Testing in School*. London: Routledge.

MCEETYA. 2008. *Melbourne Declaration on Educational Goals for Young Australians*. Edited by Ministerial Council on Education Employment Training and Youth Affairs. Melbourne: Ministerial Council on Education Employment Training and Youth Affairs.

McLaughlin, Milbrey. 2006. "Implementation Research in Education." In *New Directions in Education Policy Implementation: Confronting Complexity*, edited by M. Honig, 209–228. New York: State University of New York Press.

Miles, Mathew B., and A. Michael Huberman. 1994. *Qualitative Data Analysis*. 2nd ed. Thousand Oaks, CA: Sage.

Mockler, Nicole. 2016. "NAPLAN and the 'Problem Frame': Exploring Representations in the Print Media of NAPLAN, 2010–2013." In *National Testing in Schools*, edited by Bob Lingard, Greg Thompson, and Sam Sellar, 181–198. London: Routledge.

Nichols, S., and D. Berliner. 2007. *Collateral Damage*. Cambridge, MA: Harvard Educational Press.

Niesche, Richard. 2013. "Foucault, Counter-conduct and School Leaderships as a Form of Political Subjectivity." *Journal of Educational Administration and History* 45 (2): 144–158.

Sahlberg, S. 2011. *Finnish Lessons*. New York: Teachers College Press.

Repositioning prevention in child protection using performance indicators

Clare Tilbury

ABSTRACT
Performance indicators have both technical and value dimensions, capable of providing data for monitoring and reporting in addition to framing policy problems and their solutions. This paper considers the performance indicators proposed in a recent child protection inquiry in Australia that recommended 'decreasing the numbers of children in the child protection system' as a primary policy objective. The paper examines the context in which the indicators were set, the values and theories they endorse, and how they position stakeholders. The analysis shows how the indicators communicate that child protection services should be only for the most serious cases of child maltreatment, and the reach of statutory services should be curtailed. Children who have been maltreated or who are at risk of harm from abuse or neglect should be diverted from the child protection system (positioned as bad) to the family support system (positioned as good), and at the same time from the state to the nongovernment sector. The shifting relations between government, service providers, and families signified by the indicators can be seen in a broader international context of tightening the boundaries around child protection and concurrently advancing concepts of compliance within family support.

Introduction

When viewed instrumentally, as a technical tool to retrospectively monitor policies and programs, performance measurement is grounded in a step-wise or rational view of policy: a policy problem exists, and knowledge (in the form of quantitative data) is obtained to aid policy choices. Indicators are neutral, following the logic of the problem, and developed in pursuit of the unproblematic values of efficiency and effectiveness. According to this approach, if properly conceptualised and constructed (or valid and reliable), performance indicators can illuminate the extent to which agencies or services are achieving goals and can provide accountability internally to the next level of management and externally to stakeholders. However, the requirement for clear, uncontested policy goals in the rational policy model does not recognise that stakeholders may have different aims and perspectives, and access to different forms of power in the policy process (Considine 1994). In social policy fields such as child protection, policy goals can be ambiguous, with multiple agendas pursued simultaneously. Various policy participants have different interpretations of central values (such as the best interests of the child), and the policy process is iterative and recursive rather than logical and orderly. Notions of best practice and good outcomes are contested. Therefore, if presented as technical or neutral, performance indicators de-politicise, presenting certain policy objectives as unproblematic, as if they do not serve particular interests or represent particular views of the world (Le Gales 2011).

An alternative approach is to conceptualise performance indicators as policy instruments that carry meanings and concepts, express policy frames, and organise relations between the state and the policy actors governed by them (Lascoumes and Le Gales 2007; Le Gales 2011). Understanding performance indicators as policy instruments requires examination of their social as well as their technical capacities. The effectiveness of an indicator as a means to measure is not as important as other roles such as setting policy and structuring relations between policy participants. This approach opens up questions about who is 'performing', the interpretations that are made of data, and how the indicators explain or theorise the relationships between government and nongovernment agencies, professionals, families, and other stakeholders in a policy field. It draws attention to the discursive function of indicators in communicating policy intent, shaping the way we think and talk about child protection, and defining notions of outcomes, effectiveness, and quality (Alastalo and Poso 2014; Tilbury 2004).

Research on performance measurement in the child protection field

Child protection systems comprise a set of social policies, legislation, organisational arrangements, and professional practices to respond to child abuse and neglect. Internationally, while there is significant variation between countries, three distinct orientations for child protection systems have been identified across developed European and Anglo-American countries: categorised as child protection; family support; or child focus (Gilbert, Parton, and Skivenes 2011). The classification by Gilbert et al. considered the extent to which governments promoted child development, family support, or protection from parental abuse or neglect; whether policies were primarily targeted at social inequality or individual deviance; and how legalistic and adversarial services were. As such, they reflect distinct value orientations. Common trends were also noted over the past two decades. First, child protection was politically volatile, with intense media coverage of perceived failures in protecting individual children. Second, definitions of child abuse risks expanded, with more children coming to the attention of child protection authorities and more children in care. Third, managerial approaches to child protection increased, with new accountability and oversight mechanisms and more formal procedures and technologies for assessing and responding to children.

Performance measurement is an accountability mechanism now widely used in child protection. Much of the research on performance measurement in this field is in the rationalist mode, advancing the general view that performance measurement is a good thing, as long as the indicators are evidence-based, valid indicators of what they purport to measure and the data are available (Testa and Poertner 2010). Problems with government audits and performance improvement processes have been detailed.

These include technical and empirical problems with the limitations of available administrative data, interpreting performance data without accounting for demographic variations between localities and states, contradictions between measures whereby improvement on one inevitably leads to decline on another, arbitrary standard-setting, and potential for gaming or manipulating data (Courtney, Needell, and Wulczyn 2004). Two out-of-home care performance indicators have been the subject of considerable empirical scrutiny in Britain: placement stability and educational attainment. These are proxy child well-being indicators, measuring how frequently children are moved around from placement to placement, and how they are achieving in school compared to their peers. Research has examined whether these are the right goals to be aiming for, whether pursuing targets on these goals could undermine focus on individual children's needs, the difficulty of attribution due to the complex factors causing the problems, and the best measurement rules to apply for the indicators (Berridge 2012; Ward and Skuse 2001).

At a more conceptual level, there has been criticism that performance indicators are reductionist, too narrowly designed to measure the complexity of practice, and focused on quantity over quality, serving managerial interests rather than clients. For example, Gupta and Blewett (2007) argued that social work is about relationships with clients that are not amenable to measurement, and that many changes brought about in the lives of people receiving social work services are subtle and non-tangible, and cannot be represented as quantifiable outcomes. In existing child protection performance measurement regimes, there are few child and family outcome indicators, and a reliance on available output data (such as number of children and placements). Alastalo and Poso (2014) argued that as performance measures count and aggregate, they make their objects knowable and governable, and in doing so, simplify and mask the variation of social factors that lead to placement in out-of-home care. In representing certain policy objectives and 'best practice' standards, indicators influence how the child protection system is conceptualised, how good practice is defined, and how funds are allocated. Therefore, with the focus of performance measurement on investigation and out-of-home care (the more intrusive parts of the system) the indicators represent a narrow and reactive view of child protection (Tilbury 2004). Notably missing are measures of family needs and services, and measures of children's social and emotional well-being.

A marked shift to the process of risk assessment as a central task of child protection can be seen as a manifestation of the 'risk society' in which reduced trust in government and expert knowledge has led to a societal concern to monitor, measure, explain, and contain risks (Munro 2010). There has been a considerable critique of performance measurement's role as a tool of risk management in child protection. According to Munro (2004, 2010) performance measurement has encouraged the development of a culture of proceduralisation, blaming, deprofessionalisation, and computerisation of social work. She argued that performance audit processes in England changed over time from being a conversation about practice, to case file reviews that focused on completion of paperwork, thereby imposing an administrative burden that detracted from the amount of time social workers had to engage with children and families. Munro (2011) further argued indicators distorted practice by diverting the attention of the practitioner away from the needs of the individual client in favour of attaining output targets set by government.

This paper takes a critical and interpretive approach to examine the policy-setting functions of performance indicators. The empirical case examined is the indicators proposed by the recent Queensland Child Protection Commission of Inquiry (QCPCI). The Inquiry's recommendations provide the basis for current child protection policy directions in this State (QCPCI 2013). The analysis will consider:

- The political context in which the performance indicators were set.
- The policy frames embedded in the indicators, how they represent the problem of child abuse, and the role of the child protection system.
- The roles and responsibilities of government and nongovernment agencies, professionals, and families, and how these are demarcated in the indicators.

The context for the inquiry

As a federation, in Australia child protection is the responsibility of state governments, each with their own legislation and approaches. The 2013 QCPCI was established by a newly elected conservative state government to fulfil an election promise. Unlike many other inquiries in child protection in both Australia and England, it was not prompted by a perceived crisis or critical event. The rationale for holding the Inquiry was increasing demands on the system: the fact that there had been no apparent improvements in the child protection system despite two previous major public inquiries and large injections of funds since 2000. The Inquiry was asked to examine a suite of problems that had arisen over the last decade, depicted as follows:

- the number of reports from hospitals, police, schools and community members concerned about possible child abuse or neglect tripled;
- the number of children in care doubled;
- statutory caseloads remained too high;
- the quality of out-of-home care placements had not improved, with less stability, less cultural matching, and inadequate support for young people upon leaving care; and
- the disparity of Aboriginal and Torres Strait Islander children in care worsened, with over-representation increasing from about 25% to 40% of children in care being Indigenous (when they are 5% of the total child population).

The terms of reference for the Inquiry stated that its recommendations should take account of a major audit taking place into the state budget. This led the Inquiry to 'propose reforms that will not place a further strain on the state's finances' (QCPCI 2013, 1).

After taking evidence from government and nongovernment agencies, professionals, academics, carers, children and young people, and families, the Inquiry found that despite continual review and change, and significantly increased budgets over the past 15 years, a widespread public perception of systemic failure persisted. In order to achieve the child protection system's goals of ensuring the care and protection of children, the Inquiry made 121 recommendations to government in a report titled 'Taking responsibility: a roadmap for Queensland child protection.' There were three objectives for the roadmap: firstly, to reduce the number of children and young people in the child protection system; secondly, to revitalise frontline and family support services; and thirdly, to refocus oversight mechanisms (QCPCI 2013, 5). The performance indicators that were proposed for evaluating progress towards the first objective of reducing the number of children in the child protection system, which are the subject of this paper, are as follows:

- Performance indicator 1 (PI-1) – fewer children in out-of-home care.
- Performance indicator 2 (PI-2) – reduced rate of Aboriginal and Torres Strait Islander children in out-of-home care.
- Performance indicator 3 (PI-3) – reduced number of reports and re-reports about suspected child abuse or neglect.
- Performance indicator 4 (PI-4) – increased access to family support (QCPCI 2013, 526–527).

Defining the child protection system: the problem with diversion

In general, child protection services in Australia are residual, characterised by a 'child protection orientation' that aims to protect children from parental abuse or neglect within a legal and investigative framework, with a high threshold for state intervention (Gilbert, Parton, and Skivenes 2011). Despite policies to encourage supportive family-based responses to concerns about children, there are insufficient support services available (Lonne et al. 2009). There are very high rates of racial disparity, with Indigenous children being at least seven times more likely to be in care than non-Indigenous children, but overall not a high rate of children in out-of-home care by international standards (Tilbury 2008). The number of reports of suspected child abuse and neglect has significantly increased markedly, with most reports not meeting the required threshold for action (QCPCI 2013, 85). Broadly, the Inquiry proposed to 'divert' children and families from the coercive statutory interventions of investigation, court orders, and placement in out-of-home care, and increase access to voluntary family support services. This was based on the premise that helping families at early stages of problem development would improve outcomes for children and reduce costs later. This preventative turn is a well-rehearsed proposition in child protection in many countries, including Australia, Britain, and the Netherlands (Parton 2006; Van Nijnatten, Hopman, and Knijn 2014).

It might be argued that providing more in-home family support, reducing the number of children in care, and reducing the over-representation of Aboriginal and Torres Strait Islander children in care are worthy goals. They reinforce the principles of minimal intrusion into family life, that coercive state powers should not unduly interfere in how parents raise children, and that children have a right to family life. 'Diverting families from the statutory system' comprised a whole chapter of the Inquiry report, concluding with 13 recommendations. But the concept of diversion that underpins the performance indicators is problematic. Diversion is a policy imported from the criminal justice system, based on redirecting or turning away *from* something bad *to* something good. It is not readily transferrable to child protection. The comparison is ill-made because diverting from juvenile detention or prison is entirely different to diverting from foster care or kinship care. Detention or prison is a punishment (albeit with a rehabilitation aim) imposed by the criminal justice system; placement is not a punishment. Drawing the analogy to child protection implies children who are vulnerable should preferably be diverted from the child protection system (bad) to the family support system (good). Thus, the indicators portray statutory child protection not just as investigation-focused, procedural and bureaucratic; but also as a dangerous or harmful system for children (Van Nijnatten, Hopman, and Knijn 2014). Child protection intervention, whether an investigation of suspected abuse or neglect or placement in out-of-home care, is undertaken wholly for the benefit of the child, it is contradictory to regard it as something to be avoided. The roadmap's objective of reducing the number of children in the child protection system sits curiously at odds with the overall goal of the state to ensure the care and protection of children, as if the number of children who need protection is a financial drain on the government, rather than a vital service for vulnerable children.

Further, the premise of PI-1 and PI-2, that out-of-home care for children should be avoided, is not supported by research. Research has shown that delaying entry into care for some children may be costly in terms of longer exposure to maltreatment impairing the child's development, greater difficulty in meeting their needs, delayed permanence, and increased costs of placements (Ward and Skuse 2001). The problem with a 'goal keeping' mode of child protection, in which out-of-home care is positioned as a last resort, is that a hands-off approach can lead to a worsening of family problems then result in unplanned, crisis placements, which are ultimately more resource intensive (Packman, Randall, and Jacques 1986).

Being in care is not uniformly bad for children. Certainly, research on educational attainment, health, and well-being, shows that children in care are worse off compared to their peers, and this adversely affects their adult outcomes (Barber and Delfabbro 2005; Berridge 2012). Yet this gap cannot all be attributed to the care system, it also relates to children's pre-care experiences that delay their development. There are detrimental effects of being in care, especially from placement instability and drift in unplanned care, as children's development is adversely affected by separation from family, cultural ties, and school friends (Bullock et al. 2006). The care system could do much more to address these losses, and the lack of belonging that many children experience. While findings about outcomes for children are based on the quality of care received in the past, outcomes for children in the future could be improved with better resourced and skilled out-of-home care. The research definitely provides grounds for advocating for improvements to the quality of foster care and other care system arrangements, but it does not provide a rationale for concluding that out-of-home care should be avoided. Overall, research provides a nuanced picture of the efficacy of care, depending particularly on the age of children when they enter care, the type of placement provided, how long they stay, and the provision of after-care support (Bullock et al. 2006). And many children feel they are better off in care, feeling safe and cared for (Barber and Delfabbro 2005). Therefore, the diversion discourse misrepresents out-of-home care, conveying all the negatives of care, and few of the positives.

Child protection services are not inherently or necessarily legalistic and adversarial, they can be designed and operationalised with variable capacities to compel or empower. The performance objective of reducing the number of reports to the statutory agency (PI-3) reflects a long debate in child welfare about the proper balance between compulsory and supportive responses to child maltreatment. There are different perspectives, based partly on research and partly on changing public and professional norms about parenting and child care, regarding how much child abuse is caused by aberrant parental behaviour, or mediated by inequality and disadvantage. Many governments in recent years have been trying to ensure that the balance of resources is not weighted too heavily to compulsory interventions, which leaves insufficient resources for 'early help' and preventative family support to assist socially disadvantaged families who have many needs (Thoburn 2013).

The Inquiry defined the reporting threshold (PI-3) for entry to the statutory system with reference to the 'significant harm' threshold in the legislation, as services provided by the state when parents are unable or unwilling to protect a child. This definition provides no foundation for equating statutory services with coercive or compulsory services, to be avoided whenever possible. It is not clear why access to a service that is needed to protect a child should be restricted, or why intensive family support interventions are positioned as outside the statutory child protection system, when legislation expressly provides for family support responses to child abuse and neglect (Child Protection Act [Qld] s5, s7). In reality, by statute and via funding arrangements, the child protection system comprises much more than the work that statutory child protection officers undertake with families regarding child abuse or neglect. In-home family support interventions are provided by statutory services through both supervision orders (granted by the court to give the state authority to issue directions to a parent and supervise a child's care while living at home with parents) and a type of family preservation response (called intervention with parental agreement). Further, the principles of respect for families and family participation in case planning are accepted as crucial to good child protection practice, whether statutory or not.

The performance indicators put forward by the Inquiry counter-pose child protection and family support, as if they are separate, for different risk categories. Out-of-home care is seen essentially as a child protection rather than as a family support service. It is mostly court-ordered, and consequently placement has a stigma attached to it for both children and parents. But in some countries (such as Denmark and Finland) out-of-home care is regarded as a positive support service for those who need it, and most children are placed on a voluntary basis with parental agreement. The Inquiry's recommendations were guided by the principle that the state is the last resort for protecting and caring for children (QCPCI 2013, 9). However, State intervention can come in many forms. State intervention is necessary to protect and care for children, supplementing what parents are able to provide, because parenting is one of many factors that influence children's well-being. The provision of education, health services, and public housing are forms of state intervention that make positive contributions to child well-being. So it is not the fact of state intervention that is the problem, it is the nature of it: that the state concentrates its child protection resources on coercive interventions with families. Consequently, State child protection services are seen as stigmatising, not supportive. The inference that nothing good comes of state intervention represents a retreat from statutory child protection work as quality social work with families to protect children.

The Inquiry proposed reducing the rate of Indigenous children in care as a measure of reform success (PI-2). Certainly, data on racial disproportionality and disparity can be used to assess the quality, equity, and effectiveness of services in protecting children and helping their families. However, with the disparity gap so wide, only modest gains can be achieved through concentrating on diversion. Different rates of entry to care can be explained by risk factors for child abuse and neglect not being evenly distributed throughout the population. If proportionately more Indigenous families experience hardships and live in disadvantaged communities, then more of their children may be at risk of abuse or neglect, and their families are more likely to be in need of culturally appropriate support and practical assistance. Attention is required to the social inequalities that lead to the patterned disparities observed in child welfare, as well as health and education systems (Bywaters et al. 2014). It is more critical, and just, to address the underlying causes of family problems for Indigenous people to improve family resources and living conditions, working collaboratively with Indigenous communities. Raising the threshold for entry to care, paradoxically, is likely to exacerbate over-representation, unless accompanied by policies and services that tackle the uneven distribution of poverty and other risk factors amongst children in Australia.

The changing role of the nongovernment sector

The performance indicators also signify a change in relations between government and nongovernment sectors, extending and making overt the responsibility of community-based family support agencies to monitor families. Over many decades, nongovernment agencies (especially those with religious and charitable roots) have played a role in delivering family support in Australia (Australian Institute of Health and Welfare 2001). Performance measurement is a tool to govern these organisations, providing a means of indirect control of service delivery to manage expenditure and action when government does not directly provide services (Salamon 2002). Contract arrangements require agencies to supply quantitative data about various elements of their functioning and meet performance targets. Here, performance measures are more than a technical mechanism to monitor performance; they structure relationships between government and nongovernment providers. The agencies perform to government specifications, and in doing so, their autonomy and flexibility are regulated. Casting statutory child protection in narrow terms has particular implications for preventative family support services, because a high threshold for access to child protection services has a flow-on effect to the threshold for obtaining family support.

The concept of prevention, with accompanying differentiation between primary, secondary and tertiary levels, is malleable, because prevention programs have a governance function. They define system boundaries or eligibility thresholds in a context where rationing services is important (Freeman 1999). While escalating numbers of reports of abuse and neglect led many states to invest in family support programs, the bulk of resources have been allocated to services targeting families with serious concerns about child maltreatment (Tomison 2002). There has been minimal expansion in broader, truly secondary-level family support for families experiencing moderate difficulty. Even so, intensive family support remains a small part of the child protection system, comprising only 17% of total State and Territory governments spending on child welfare in 2014 (SCRGSP 2015, Table 15A.1). The consequence of insufficient support services to meet the needs of families is higher thresholds, and more restrictive criteria for access to assistance.

Increased access to family support (PI-4) is to be achieved by priority being given to families reported to child protection. Family support becomes 'semi-voluntary' and more conditional (Hayden and Jenkins 2014). This is another sign of the changing role of the state represented in the indicators, whereby the criteria for receipt of state services become more restrictive, and the community sector has an increased role. The performance indicators are not forming a new market, because family support has long been provided in the community sector, but it is remodelling the family support market, requiring it to provide different types of 'products' or services. This reframes the idea of early intervention. While family support represents a move away from coercive services and provides for a more active role for families, the reframing also positions family support as having a stronger role in the governance of the family and the oversight of parenting.

Along with the changed role of the family support sector comes the necessity for more personal information about families to be exchanged between government and nongovernment agencies to facilitate referrals. Parton (2006) has observed that the current preventative shift is accompanied by development of new forms of information technology for recording and sharing information about families. These prevention programs involve large-scale screening and monitoring of risk, and exchange of information between designated professionals and between agencies. He argued that this approach to prevention makes the state more intrusive, more regulatory, with professionals (in children's services, police and health services) having increased responsibility and powers to intervene, and not only when a child has been abused or neglected, or there is risk of significant harm to a child. There is potential here for breaching privacy and undermining civil liberties, especially of people in 'risk categories'.

A further shift from government to nongovernment provision is embedded in the goal to decrease the number of reports about suspected child abuse or neglect to child protection authorities (PI-3) by implementing a community-based referral pathway. The objective of this indicator is contrary to at least three decades of public policy and legislation that has directed certain categories of professionals (teachers, doctors) to report suspected child abuse and neglect. Now government wants them to step back, because of the magnitude of the workload caused by the number of reports it receives. The Inquiry recommended that unless children were in immediate or serious danger, reporters should be encouraged to refer their concerns to a community agency rather than to the statutory agency, through the implementation of community-based intake (QCPCI 2013, recommendation 4.5). This inevitably leaves the indicators open to manipulation if the same total number of reports is made, because improvement on the indicator can be achieved by government redirecting reporters to an alternative (government-funded) community agency for screening and assessment. Moreover, having an alternative pathway for reporters does not in itself provide early intervention and support for families, which can only be achieved by having a sufficient number and range of services available. The nongovernment sector will have to manage the needs of families and the expectations of reporters within the funding allocations and contract arrangements that regulate their flexibility.

Role of children and families

Where is the voice of children, young people, and their families, how are they positioned as they are diverted from statutory services? There were no performance indicators proposed by the Inquiry to measure child and family views of services or whether services make a difference to them. The family support indicator (PI-4) does not refer to empowering or providing assistance to parents, it is about access to family support services. Funding is recommended for intensive family support services that give priority to 'high-risk' families with multiple and complex needs in order to achieve diversion from statutory intervention (QCPCI 2013, recommendation 5.4). Following a referral expressing concern about the care of a child, such services seek the 'agreement' of families to receive services. Accepting services is equated with caring for their children; the family has to accede to the intervention to show their willingness to improve their situation. The voluntary notion is further eroded as families understand if they do not 'agree to participate' in services, child protection may step in. There is a compliance element here because as families are being governed, parents must perform for professionals. There is no allowance that services might be difficult to access, or not what families want, families must submit to services or face the prospect of more intrusive intervention. Parents are perceived as being not motivated, hostile, or resistant without due consideration to the power that professionals hold, or the fears that parents may have about child protection intervention. Thus, on the surface the preventative approach is empowering for families, but it also has a controlling element of identifying future risk and risky parents (Featherstone, White, and Morris 2014; Van Nijnatten, Hopman, and Knijn 2014).

The categorical approach that sets service delivery options in opposition – statutory versus voluntary and child protection versus family support – implies there is no overlap between their goals and target clientele. That is, family support is for parents who access and participate in programs, who are not aggressive, difficult or uncooperative, and child protection is for parents who lack motivation to change, who would not 'help themselves', who decline offers of help or are evasive. In reality, there is no clear distinction between the needs of families who receive a child protection service and families who receive a family support response. In selecting a response to concerns about children, much depends upon what services are available. And both these service types contain levels of voluntariness – for example, short-term placements or respite care are a type of family support service that parents may seek in a crisis. Linking access to family support (PI-4) to the policy goal of diversion is consistent with the international trend of tightening the boundaries around child protection and concurrently advancing concepts of compliance within family support. It reinforces and intensifies the idea of family support as semi-voluntary, contrasting it with (coercive) child protection. It also casts family participation as entirely a decision for the parents, rather than as part of the skill repertoire of child protection practitioners and their capacity to engage with families, building rapport and trust, and using their professional power in a nuanced and productive manner.

The diversion goal and associated performance indicators contain an explanation for child maltreatment that is about individual parents 'taking responsibility'. This frames the care and protection of children in terms of the skills and resources of parents: if they access family support and repair their problems, they can avoid coercive child protection intervention. In doing so, it downplays the impact of social conditions, poverty, homelessness, racism, unemployment, disability, and ill-health. This policy direction of favouring individual over social responsibility is not confined to child protection; it is a characteristic of neoliberal welfare regimes (Gilbert, Parton, and Skivenes 2011). Yet holding people responsible for their behaviour is not contrary to recognising the environmental factors that can generate and sustain the problematic behaviour. Howe (1996) described this as a focus on surface over depth: rather than trying to theorise (that is, understand or explain), social workers focus on observable behaviour, less concerned with *why* clients behave as they do than with *what* they do. Social arrangements and social exclusion, the availability of jobs, housing, child care, family support, and school inclusiveness are downplayed while parental behaviours related to domestic violence, mental illness, or using alcohol or drugs are targeted as the crucial determinant of children's well-being. As Valentine (2015) argues, whereas the concept of social exclusion describes the social processes that exclude, the concept of multi-problem families refers to the characteristics of families and signifies it is the families who need changing. Despite understanding that the causes of child abuse and neglect are both social and individual, all the prevention action is directed at individual behaviours or parenting practices, rather than social circumstances. A punitive approach is then taken towards parents, in the name of being child-centred (Featherstone, White, and Morris 2014). Therefore, the indicators define and identify good and bad parents according to their behaviours.

The consequences – what is measured is valued

There are technical problems with the indicators that arise from framing child protection in narrow terms, as a system from which children should be diverted. Firstly, they are indicators of service system outputs, attaching importance to quantity rather than quality. None of them are outcome or quality indicators, they do not measure improvements in children's safety or well-being, or enhancements in family functioning. Some are contradictory. For example, there is a fundamental contradiction in regarding out-of-home placement as undesirable, when it is done to protect the child. Perverse outcomes can result from avoiding placing a child who is not safe at home, or returning a child home prematurely to reduce numbers in care. Also, there is an inverse relationship between the rate of entry to care and placement quality. Lowering the rate of entry (by raising the threshold) so that only the most serious cases enter out-of-home care (PI-1), means that placement stability will decline, because it is harder to maintain placements in which children have emotional or behavioural problems. In fact, the rate of entries to care has been declining in Queensland for many years, as it is in the rest of Australia and many other countries (Australian Institute of Health and Welfare 2015; Gilbert, Parton, and Skivenes 2011). The reason there are more children in care is that duration in care has increased, so there are more children in care year-on-year (Tilbury, 2008). This is a long-term trend that can only turn around if more reunification work is done. Increasing access to family support at the early stages is necessary, but not nearly sufficient, to reduce the number of children in care. Finally, there is no sound evidence base for the indicators. For example, there is no basis in research for setting a standard about the right rate of children in care (PI-1 and PI-2). Both 'too high' and 'too low' levels can be problematic: a low number of children being removed from their birth families can arise from either skilled help making the children safe, or from poor-quality risk assessments (Tilbury 2008; Munro 2004).

Conclusion

Understanding the performance indicators set by the QCPCI as a policy instrument facilitates an exploration of how they frame child protection policy and affect relations between government, service providers, and service users. The performance indicators communicate that child protection services should be only for the most serious cases of child maltreatment, statutory services are characterised as coercive, and the goal is to reduce the reach of statutory services. Children who are vulnerable should be diverted from the (narrowly defined) child protection system to the family support system and from the state to the community sector. In doing so, the performance indicators reposition prevention within the child protection system, moving family support from a voluntary service for families at the early stages of problem development, to a more conditional service. That is, families must cooperate with services and reduce their problem behaviours to avoid coercive intervention. This approach also repositions nongovernment family support agencies to become an agent of the smaller state, with referrals channelled to them from child protection and other government agencies. While these trends in service delivery have been perceptible over time, because the performance indicators are policy instruments that command resources, they elevate and make the policy objectives explicit, and intensify policy action towards them.

According to Power (2004, 778), the task of social science is to 'open up the black box of performance measurement systems, to de-naturalise them and to recover the social and political work that has gone into their construction as instruments of control'. This paper has considered the consequences of setting performance indicators that are directed towards reducing the number of children in the child protection system. In constructing child protection policy, it matters what type of family services are provided, to whom, by whom, and how statutory child protection and its practitioners are viewed. Performance information should not be treated as a straightforward or neutral measure of policy action, but interrogated to see what lies behind it, and the implications for government, the nongovernment sector, and families. The indicators discussed in this paper are consistent with an international trend of tightening the boundaries around child protection, and concurrently advancing concepts of compliance within family support. An alternative scenario is to conceptualise the child protection system as a positive service that helps vulnerable and multiply disadvantaged families. Parents need services that genuinely help them with caring for their children and managing family stress, with sufficient intensity and levels of support, attending to both personal agency and structural inequalities that affect family life. Sometimes the services might be in-home, other times placement is needed. These services contain different levels of voluntariness and should not be positioned at opposite ends of a continuum.

Disclosure statement

No potential conflict of interest was reported by the authors.

References

Alastalo, M., and T. Poso. 2014. "Number of Children Placed Outside the Home as an Indicator: Social and Moral Implications of Commensuration." *Social Policy and Administration* 48 (7): 721–738.

Australian Institute of Health and Welfare. 2001. *Family Support Services in Australia 2000*. Canberra: Australian Institute of Health and Welfare.
Australian Institute of Health and Welfare. 2015. *Child Protection Australia 2013-2014*. Canberra: Australian Institute of Health and Welfare.
Barber, J., and P. Delfabbro. 2005. "Children's Adjustment to Long-Term Foster Care." *Children and Youth Services Review* 27: 329-340.
Berridge, D. 2012. "Educating Young People in Care: What have We Learned?" *Children and Youth Services Review* 34: 1171-1175.
Bullock, R., M. E. Courtney, R. Parker, I. Sinclair, and J. Thoburn. 2006. "Can the Corporate State Parent?" *Children and Youth Services Review* 28: 1344-1358.
Bywaters, P., G. Brady, T. Sparks, and E. Bos. 2014. "Child Welfare Inequalities: New Evidence, Further Questions." *Child and Family Social Work*, Advance online publication. doi:10.1111/cfs.12154.
Considine, M. 1994. *Public Policy: A Critical Approach*. Melbourne: MacMillan.
Courtney, M. E., B. Needell, and F. Wulczyn, 2004. "Unintended Consequences of the Push for Accountability: The Case of National Child Welfare Performance Standards." *Children and Youth Services Review* 26: 1141-1154.
Featherstone, B., S. White, and K. Morris, 2014. *Re-imagining Child Protection: Towards Humane Social Work with Families*. Bristol: Policy Press.
Freeman, R. 1999. "Recursive Politics: Prevention, Modernity and Social Systems." *Children and Society* 13: 232-241.
Gilbert, N., N. Parton, and M. Skivenes. 2011. *Child Protection Systems: International Trends and Orientations*. New York: Oxford University Press.
Gupta, A., and J. Blewett. 2007. "Change for Children? The Challenges and Opportunities for the Children's Social Work Workforce." *Child and Family Social Work* 12 (2): 172-181.
Hayden, C., and C. Jenkins. 2014. "'Troubled Families' Programme in England: 'Wicked Problems'. and Policy-Based Evidence." *Policy Studies* 35 (6): 631-649.
Howe, D. 1996. "Surface and Depth in Social Work Practice." In *Social Theory, Social Change and Social Work*, edited by N. Parton, 77-97. London: Routledge.
Lascoumes, P., and P. Le Gales. 2007. "Introduction: Understanding Public Policy through its Instruments – From the Nature of Instruments to the Sociology of Public Policy Instrumentation." *Governance: An International Journal of Policy, Administration, and Institutions* 20 (1): 1-21.
Le Gales, P. 2011. "Policy Instruments and Governance." In *The SAGE Handbook of Governance*, edited by M. Bevir, 142-160, ch. 20. London: Sage.
Lonne, B., N. Parton, J. Thomson, and M. Harries. 2009. *Reforming Child Protection*. London: Routledge.
Munro, E. 2004. "The Impact of Audit on Social Work Practice." *British Journal of Social Work* 34 (8): 1075-1095.
Munro, E. 2010. "Learning to Reduce Risk in Child Protection." *British Journal of Social Work* 40: 1135-1151.
Munro, E. 2011. *The Munro Review of Child Protection: Final Report – A child-centred System*. London: Department for Education.
Packman, J., Randall, J., and Jacques, N. 1986. *Who Needs Care? Social Work Decisions about Children*. Oxford: Basil Blackwell.
Parton, N. 2006. *Safeguarding Childhood: Early Intervention and Surveillance in a Late Modern Society*. Basingstoke: Palgrave Macmillan.
Power, M. 2004. "Counting, Control and Calculation: Reflections on Measuring and Management." *Human Relations* 57 (6): 765-783.
QCPCI (Queensland Child Protection Commission of Inquiry). 2013. *Taking Responsibility: A Roadmap for Queensland Child Protection*. Brisbane: Queensland Child Protection Commission of Inquiry.
Salamon, L. M. 2002. *The Tools of Government: A Guide to the New Governance*. Oxford: Oxford University Press.

SCRGSP (Steering Committee for the Review of Government Service Provision). 2015. *Report on Government Services 2015*. Canberra: Productivity Commission.
Testa, M. F., and Poertner, J., eds. 2010. *Fostering Accountability: Using Evidence to Guide and Improve Child Welfare Policy*. New York: Oxford University Press.
Thoburn, J. 2013. "Troubled Families, Troublesome Families, and the Trouble with Payment by Results." *Families, Relationships and Societies* 2 (3): 471–475.
Tilbury, C. 2004. "The influence of performance measurement on child welfare." *British Journal of Social Work*, 34 (2): 225–241.
Tilbury, C., and J. Thoburn 2008. "Children in out-of-home care in Australia: international comparisons." *Children Australia*, 33 (3): 5–12.
Tomison, A. M. 2002. "Preventing Child Abuse: Changes to Family Support in the 21st Century." *Child Abuse Prevention Issues* 17: 1–22.
Valentine, k. 2015. "Complex Needs and Wicked Problems: How Social Disadvantage Became Multiple." *Social Policy and Society*. Advance online doi:10.1017/S1474746415000342.
Van Nijnatten, C., M. Hopman, and T. Knijn. 2014. "Child Protection Victims and the 'Evil Institutions'." *Social Sciences* 3 (4): 726–741.
Ward, H., and T. Skuse. 2001. "Performance Targets and Stability of Placements for Children Long Looked After Away from Home." *Children and Society* 15 (5): 333–346.

Legislation

CPA 1999 *Child Protection Act 1999* (QLD).

Techniques and paradoxes in performing performance measurements: concluding reflections

Paul Henman

ABSTRACT
Performance measurement has an implicit performance theory embedded within its practice; performance measurement perforce performs. Performance measurement has a performative effect on performance. Drawing together and building on the various empirical observations from the preceding papers in this collection, this concluding paper firstly examines the circumstances in which performance measurement performs, that is, when it produces 'authentic' performance improvements, compared to when performance measurements misfire. The paper secondly explores several paradoxes of performance measurement – such that performance measurement measures only part of the performance it seeks to be performative on, incentives to perform incentivise poor performance and so on. These paradoxes, contradictions and ironies must be apprehended and appreciated in discovering, discerning and deciphering the diverse dynamics of measuring performance. They also demonstrate that analysing and working with performance measurement requires a perspective that eschews absolutes and clear directions, and embraces the uneasy and potentially destabilising tension of Escher's performative art.

Ontology and *episteme* of performance measurement

Performance measurement is a technology, a tool, a device. More specifically it is an information technology, in that it both generates data and is data. It is also a technology of government (or governance) (cf. Miller and Rose 2008, 63–65), in that its purpose is to use data to govern, manage or steer the objects of performance and/or the actors that contribute to that performance. This special edition of *Policy Studies* has framed performance measurement using the policy instrument approach (see Lascoumes and Le Galès 2007; Le Galès 2011; Le Galès 2016) because of its ability to capture this technology perspective of performance measurement.

As Le Galès and Lascoumes' work emphasise, taking such an approach puts the mechanism and practice of performance measurement at the centre of analysis, rather than as a technical mechanism within a wider performance problem. As such, it forces a critical gaze on that tool – how it is formed and what it does – rather than treating it as part of the furniture or background of the research object. While technical questions of performance measurement – what to measure, how to measure, how often, by whom and how to use measurement data – remain of analytical importance, they are also socio-political questions that are largely out of the scope in technical considerations. Rather than asking 'how can performance measurement be made to "work" to achieve performance?', we instead ask 'what does performance measurement do to people, organisations, governing processes and the state?'. This perspective also seeks to apprehend performance measurement as having a social life and history (Law, Ruppert, and Savage 2011). The empirical studies herein have all emphasised the latter foci of analysis over the former.

The perspective offered by the policy instrument approach – namely, to treat performance measurement as a socio-technological device – helps to critically engage in a widespread tendency in both popular and academic discourse to treat technologies uncritically, dichotomously and uni-dimensionally. For example, when I tell people about my research on government's use of technology they often ask 'is it for the better or the worse?' The reality, in contrast, is that the dynamics of technology are multiple and complex, even before seeking a normative stance. New technologies are often treated dichotomously as either angels of utopia or harbingers of doom. Moreover, technologies are often conceptualised as (ontologically, politically and ethically) neutral things, and what matters is how they are used by people. This is essentially the view underpinning the adage 'guns don't kill people, bad people kill people'. Rather, it is essential to understand that technologies do things and do so quasi-independently of humans, and they encode ways of knowing and revealing the world (Winner 1980; Verbeek 2010).

Bringing these ideas and perspectives together, one approach to public sector performance measurement sees it as a new mechanism to enhance public sector performance, service quality, accountability and professionalism. Whereas a not uncommon critical social science reaction to public sector performance measurement is to treat it as a tool of neo-liberal managerialism, in which professionals have their traditional autotomy and discretion curtailed (Ball 2003; Wastell et al. 2010). While each perspectives hold helpful insights, they are too rigid to appreciate the multiple, complex and subtle reconfigurations of the public sector consequent to deploying performance measurement. Such a dichotomy also tends to shut down the transference of insights between the camps that want applied insights to enhance public sector performance and accountability, and those that see it only in terms of colonisation of managerial power.

In progressing a more nuanced and nimble engagement, this paper presents and engages with a series of dualities and paradoxes in examining public sector performance measurement. Rather than seeking a clear resolution, I argue we need to accept the tension and ambiguity, just as Escher's artwork challenges us to apprehend and appreciate what cannot be resolved. This also means that there are no easy answers, only ongoing challenges to find dynamic pathways between the spaces constructed between poles and dualities.

Performing the *techne* of performance measurement

As was observed in the introductory chapter of this special edition, public sector use of performance measurement performs a technical function. It provides a measurement of performance, which in turn provides information and knowledge about performance levels and dynamics, and in turn is both a means and a basis for performance improvement via performance governance. Putting aside a critical perspective of this machinery-like articulation of performance measurement for a moment, such a framework necessarily generates a raft of technical questions about what is to be measured, how it is to be measured, how performance is calibrated, how to interpret performance numbers and how to use these to enhance (measured) performance. These are important questions, particularly when considering the personal and organisational dynamics of performers and performance managers and their capacity to eschew, elide, ignore and game performance measurement and performance management processes.

In comparing, contrasting and reflecting on the empirical dimensions of the papers in this edition, some observations can be made about the circumstances in which performance measurement can generate *authentic* performance improvements. I say 'authentic', because improved *measured* performance does not necessarily equate to improved performance for multiple reasons. The observed circumstances that foster performance enhancement are as follows.[1]

Clarity

The area, domain or focus of performance measurement and what is to be improved needs to be clearly understood, and the purpose for measuring that domain clear. Abstract concepts, such as 'quality' or 'satisfaction' or 'learning' do not lend themselves to clarity, and as such create a vast space for confusion and contestation about what the focus of performance is about. Such abstract concepts are also often associated with multiple objectives for measuring performance, including accountability and transparency, choice and trust. Such multiple rationales for performance measurement similarly generate confusion and contestation and actors going in different directions. The papers on national well-being (Howard and Chambers 2016) and educational performance (Gable and Lingard 2016) nicely document the problematics and dynamics of nebulous concepts. The two papers on population health provide very different examples of this phenomenon. Willing's paper showed how population health performance measurement in New Zealand was clearly focused on infectious disease control which directly relates to immunisation coverage. In contrast, Foster et al.'s paper shows how population health performance in Australia was moribund by uncertainty about what aspects of population health to focus on. Similarly, Tilbury's paper demonstrates the incoherence of organisational performance indicators in child protection vis-à-vis systemic outcomes for children.

Accuracy

Performance measures must be designed to provide an accurate assessment of the focus of performance. In other words, it must have construct validity. The issue of accuracy is closely related to clarity; they go hand in hand. As in the case of national well-being (Howard and Chambers 2016), if you do not have clarity then it becomes very difficult to identify accurate measures. At the same time if you have accuracy without clarity, then the focus of the measurement is open to the debate about the appropriate measurement. Willing's paper on immunisation showed strong construct validity, whereas Australia's school performance measurement, NAPLAN, suffered considerable problems in relating aggregate student NAPLAN results to teacher, schools and systems given that student educational performance is not readily attributable to teachers and schools. Hence the need to introduce a mediating variable, namely ICSEA (Henman and Gable 2015; Gable and Lingard 2016).

Agreement

Clarity and accuracy are important design questions, but if there is no agreement or support from those whose performance is measured and managed, then performance improvement is unlikely to follow. Foster et al. demonstrate this occurring in the way General Practitioners' (GPs) stated commitment with population health goals, but rejected the involvement of Medicare Locals in shaping their professional practice. Meanwhile, Willing's account of immunisation in New Zealand showed a strong support from GPs as well as active participation in immunising children in their practice. The question of agreement also relates to practices of resistance or ignoring performance data, intentional or otherwise.

Performance chains

The capacity to produce and attribute performance statistics to all actors within a performance space is critical for performance governance. Performance statistics need to be able to be disaggregated to individual cases – be it students or professionals – and aggregated to attribute performance to a system – such as a state or nation. If performance data are not available for individual actors that 'make up' performance, then performance governance is interrupted. The seemingly seamless capacity to aggregate and disaggregate performance data from micro to macro is evidenced in New Zealand's immunisation coverage (Willing 2016) and in school performance (Gable and Lingard 2016), but not possible in Medicare Locals' regional data (Foster et al. 2016), where community health outcomes could not be directly related to individual General Practices, or in national well-being measures (Howard and Chambers 2016). In addition to technical and institutional challenges of data design and flows, political power is often an important factor of whether performance chains can be created. Performance chains are also destabilised when multiple (otherwise valid) performance measures are utilised or combined into a single measure. Multiple measures potentially creates competing and conflictual performance systems, while combined measures detach the performance data further from the performance phenomenon being measured.

Not high stakes

Classical approaches to performance measurement are based on rational choice and classical economic models that require incentives and/or disincentives to encourage/discourage good/poor performance. Such incentives/disincentives are often financial, but can also be about social standing, status or stigma, and promotion or demotion. However, too much of a good thing can be harmful, as much of the commentary on high stakes testing in schooling testifies (Amrein and Berliner 2002). The papers suggest that a balance is required to achieve performance outcomes. Too high stakes creates greater incentives for fraudulent gaming, too low does not incentivise. For example, in Australia's private, market-based primary health care sector, financial incentives are required to get traction. However, Willing's case of childhood immunisation showed that no financial rewards, but collaborative competition involving sharing of knowledge, was successful in delivering improvements in immunisation coverage. Significantly, the system was not a win–lose arrangement, where winners take from losers. It also meant that without the high stakes, actors can experiment without the fear of high cost failure. Such systems can also play on intrinsic, rather than extrinsic, rewards, which is also at the heart of 'agreement' mentioned above.

Publication

An important dynamic in obtaining traction with performance actors is to ensure performance data are published in a way that performers are linked to audiences outside their immediate surrounds. This may not necessarily require full publication to the public, but it importantly requires publication to other people to whom performers are responsive. Publication enhances incentives (as long as it does not become high stakes) by use of what Le Galés refers to 'audience democracy' and through comparative and ranking competitions.

Mechanisms and achievability

Authentic performance improvement is also more likely when there are identifiable mechanisms for performance improvement. In other words, people know how they might improve performance, or know how they can do it in the context of their other professional duties and objectives. If it is unclear how improvements can be achieved, then people are much more likely to resort to gaming the measure or resort to other deflecting tactics such as blame avoidance (Hood 2007). Indeed, requiring people to enhance their performance without the mechanisms and means by which to do so is organisational or systemic bullying.

People as individuals

The above dimensions link organisational, technical and individual circumstances and open up (or close down) the conditions of possibility for performance improvement. The final element of the equation are people. People will be people. No matter how we design a performance measurement and governance system, people react differently to the same circumstances and situations. Some naturally have high personal integrity and some are inherent gamesters, or as Le Grand observed there are knights, knaves and pawns (1997). More specifically, Bevan and Hood (2006, 522–523) articulated four different modes of response to performance measurement practices: saints; honest triers; reactive gamers and rational maniacs. Saints are ones who have a strong professional or public service ethos and will operate inconsistently with the performance measurement if seen in conflict with their ethos. Honest triers refocus their professional activities towards the broader goal encapsulated by the performance measures. Reactive gamers also support the broader goals of those enacted through the performance regime, but will game the system if they have the reason and capacity to do so. While rational maniacs do not share the performance regime goals and 'aim to manipulate data to conceal their operations' (523).

Paradoxes of performance measurement

Discussion in the above section alludes to the interplay and tensions between different poles of performance measurement. These dynamics at times also create places of paradox, to which we now turn. The playful posturing that follows has a purpose of destabilising fixed positions and categories, in order to ensure the creative tension remains in performing performance measurement. There is an array of tensions, contradictions and ironies in performing performance measurement that must be apprehended and appreciated in discovering, discerning and deciphering the diverse dynamics of measuring performance. Analysing and working with performance measurement necessarily requires a perspective that eschews absolutes and clear directions, and embraces the uneasy and potentially destabilising tension of Escher's performative art.

Performance measurements perforce performs

Performance measurement has an implicit performance theory embedded within its practice; performance measurement perforce performs. Yet this performance is paradoxical. On the one hand measurement is couched as an inert external activity that does not change the substance being measured, yet at the same time such measurement constitutes both performer and performance. Moreover, performance measurement is not typically conducted as information, but to bear upon performance; it has a performative effect on performance.

Let us draw out the argument more slowly. Measurement is typically conceived as an inert objective practice. It subjects a phenomenon to an assessment of a quality. A ruler assesses length or distance, scales assess weight or mass, thermometers assess temperature, clocks measure time (Thompson 1967) and *ipso facto* performance measurement measures performance. In doing so, the realist account of measurement considers this act of assessment independent of the object of measurement. Measuring does not change the entity. The thing is not engaged, it is objectified by measurement.

Such a perspective is partial and problematic, as research in the social studies of science and technology have revealed (Latour and Woolgar 2013). Rather, the process of measuring constitutes and creates a quality of the object. Measuring gives an entity a length, weight, temperature, duration or performance. A phenomenon now has a quality. In other words, there is no performance without performance measurement. The realist perspective is also problematic because the more abstract process of making a measuring device – a ruler, scales, thermometer or clock – or even the category of the device – feet or metres, kilograms or pounds, degrees, seconds – creates a new phenomenon; height, weight, temperature and time (Thompson 1967). This is the case when a means for measuring population health (Foster et al. 2016; Willing 2016), national well-being (Howard and Chambers 2016), a good functioning child protection service (Tilbury 2016) and so on are created. These measures of performance have embedded politics about how to numerate and categorise a phenomenon (Alonso and Starr 1989; Bowker and Star 2000; Busch 2011). The measuring instrument not only constitutes a performance (by assessing its quantity), but also what it is to perform (Law 2004; Law, Ruppert, and Savage 2011).

The realist perspective on performance measurement is also problematic as the practice of performance measurement of social subjects is not inert in a further way. When people are aware they are being measured or aware of their measured performance, people change. They engage with the measurement – they often change their behaviour and/or contest the measurement and the measuring process/device. Indeed, in many situations, this is indeed the intention of performance measuring, for performance governing. In summary, performance measurement enacts performance in multiple ways.

To increase performance we measure only a part

A second paradox is that we typically want to increase performance, but measure only a part of what it means to perform. Performance measures do not measure performance; but partially measure performance. Performance measures are therefore proxies for performance (Blastland and Dilnot 2009, Chap. 6). This is clearly evident in Gable and Lingard's paper where the quality of teachers and schools is designated by measuring students' ability in five literacy and numeracy areas yet education and learning are much broader concepts and cover many diverse topics. Tilbury also shows how the performance measurement of a child protection system says little about whether the system is performing in what Ministers and the public might understand it to mean, such as reduced numbers and levels of children at risk, or occasions of harm, or improvements in the quality of out of home care, or even the quality of life for children in and exiting out of home care.

Yet, at the same time if we try to construct a measurement of the performance objective in full (be it, 'quality' or 'excellence' or 'well-being'), we become overwhelmed with the nebulousness of the concept, its necessary inability to be numerated, the quality *qua* quality, then measuring becomes multiform, mixed up and meaningless. This is well illustrated in Howard and Chambers' paper where the concept of national well-being eludes its measurement in numbers. In short, performance measurement requires a Goldilocks judgement balancing simplicity, specificity, superficiality and summatively.

A careful reader may have observed a contradiction in the preceding discussion. On the one hand I have argued that performance measurement constitutes performance, but on the other hand I have also argued that there is a performance phenomenon beyond what is measured. This tension in what is the 'real' is at the heart of much debate within social studies of scientific knowledge, about trying to avoid naïve empirical realism while simultaneously eschewing social solipsism (Callon and Latour 1992).

Moreover, when measuring (a part of) performance we concurrently bring to the light and fore certain types of questions and problematisations of the performance which are knowable and analysable from the performance data. They also marginalise, overshadow or reinforce the ignorance of other issues, which may have been previously asked and considered, but are now displaced as they are not under the purview of the performance measurement, or issues that remain unknowable and unanalysable until measured.

Performance objectives displace policy objectives

This need for partiality for performance measurement to perform, in turn means that measuring policy objectives to generate policy outcomes are always partial; they typically do not capture the full raft of what public and social policy is expected to achieve, particularly in a partisan or multifarious policy space. At the same time, the setting of performance measurements for policy objectives focuses actors' attention on the latter instead of the former; measured performance as proxy performance actually becomes the performance. Achieving measured literacy and numeracy scores becomes educational and teaching quality (Gable and Lingard 2016) and reduced children in out of home care becomes the measure of children at risk (Tilbury 2016). In what becomes a walled world of mirrors or hyper-reality where the simulation is the real (Baudrillard 1983), what is performance measured is what is performed and what is regarded as performance.

Taken further, the policy objectives deigned by performance measurement displace policy design and a consideration of what generates policy outcomes. Managers are to manage by numbers, not by an understanding of the production of policy performance. Performance numbers invisibilises the changes that matter.

Measuring misses the dark matter of performance

If, like Neo in *The Matrix* movies, we maintain that there is a performance 'reality' outside what is measured, what I have previously phrased 'authentic' performance, then we need to accept that there is a 'dark matter' of performance. Just as cosmologists accept that there is material stuff that is beyond what is knowable, viewable and measurable that creates the knowable universe (namely dark matter), there is also material stuff outside of what is knowable, viewable and measurable outside of performance measurement that makes performance work. The parallels are multiple, organisational scholars know that organisations work not by, but in spite of, formal organisational rules: that organisations would not function if not for the rules; computers often fail to automate routines without human support; and society is more than humans (Latour 1992). Users of performance measurement to govern performance need to appreciate the subtle difference between what makes performance and what makes performance numbers, but too often such managers of performance are also lost in *The Matrix* where the numbers also designate their performance and have no interest in busting the bubble of blissful ignorance.

Publication both enables and inhibits performance

In the first half of the paper it was argued that publication of performance data provides an important dynamic for translating performance measurement into performance change. However, the public visibility of performance data can also undermine the achievement of enhanced performance because it greatly politicises the performance and associated performance regime whereby those against the regime can generate greater traction against it. The enrolment of performance actors into the regime is crucial.

Data traces are mobile, but their context is not

Performance measurement is a process that produces numbers. Too often the process of performance measurement production is regarded as unproblematic. The numbers are objective, inviolable. Yet, those numbers are typically produced through complex social, technical and organisational processes. As such the numbers reflect the circumstances of their production, whether it be through creative or fraudulent account keeping (Gao 2009), teaching to the test (Volante 2004), the socio-economic circumstances of different communities (Henman and Gable 2015), and so on. This complex social production of numbers is embedded in a precise number. Once enumerated, the number acts alone. It is a stand in, an account or trace of that performance that can take flight and float away from the circumstances of its production. It can be combined, compared and calculated in clever ways, and the case of its construction is excised. Users and interpreters of performance numbers typically have no insight into this production process, either in general or specifically, so have little appreciation of the basis on which performance (numbers) was performed. Managers then act on performance numbers *qua* numbers, not on the performance the numbers perform. It is worthwhile remembering how well that went with Collateralised Debt Obligations in the global financial crisis (Crotty 2009). In short, we must remember what American novelist Michael Ventura quipped: 'Without context, a piece of information is just a dot. It floats in your brain with a lot of other dots and doesn't mean a damn thing. Knowledge is information-in-context – connecting the dots'.

Performance measurement increases and decreases trust

Performance measurement is intrinsically part of the audit society (Power 1997), a technology by which the public sector is to be made accountable to the public. One reoccurring theme for introducing performance measurement into the public sector is to increase public trust in it. By demonstrating that public expenditure is well spent, that public services are open and accountable and not hiding anything, and by measuring performance to increase public sector performance, public trust can increase (Fard and Rostamy 2007).

Yet, this penchant for giving accounts can also erode trust in multiple ways. Firstly, in asking people to account for their performance there can be a sense that there is a lack of trust in their performance or ability to perform. This is especially the case of professionals who typically have a level of professional autonomy and discretion associated with being a professional, whereby accountability is to their professional peers and associations, not managers or the public (see Foster et al.'s 2016 for an example of the medical profession). Secondly, the act of publishing performance data generates a dynamic of comparison, ranking and league tables, which in turn readily leads to questions of why certain performers are not performing as well as others, thereby further reducing trust. Thirdly, the intensification of performance governance can generate mistrust that increases in measured performance are 'inauthentic', a result of gaming or misrepresentation, or at the cost of other valued (but perhaps unmeasured) aspects of public satisfaction or expectation. Public trust is a tricky performance trick (Grimmelikhuijsen and Meijer 2014).

Incentives are needed, but change measured performance

Performance incentives are also a tricky performance trick. If there is no dis/incentive to perform there is no performance. Why would performers bother to change what they do without an incentive, be it intrinsic or extrinsic? Yet paradoxically if there is too much dis/incentive, there is also no improved performance. As observed in the first half of this paper, high stakes performance dis/incentives generate greater incentive to manufacture performance measures unconnected to performance. This operates by extrinsic incentives displacing intrinsic ones, and rewards replaces risks. In short, poor dis/incentives create poor performance. Again, Goldilocks must be found.

Those against performance measurement are for it

Performance measurement creates a rationality of governing, or governmentality (Dean 2010), that has an internally coherent and driving logic that makes it hard to think outside of. Performance governance creates a self-fulfilling rationality spiral of 'performance' and 'measurement'. In trying to contest or problematise performance measurement, one immediately is asked if they are against the need to measure performance and to be accountable to such. Accordingly, the ground of contestation becomes one of what the performance object should be, how to measure it, and the proper interpretation and use of performance data, and how to do it better. As a consequence, those who contest performance measurement become drawn into a contestation within the parameters of the rationality of performance measurement governance. There appears to be no outside, nothing outside the matrix of performance.

Fatal remedies

As a consequence of the above constellation of dynamics, tensions and paradoxes – incentives that create no performance change, numbers that elide context and erode trust, measurements that mismeasure performance, the design of policy by numbers and a search for solutions within the rational performance measurement frame – fatal remedies can readily result. Performance measurement practices can proliferate in response to partial measures of performance. Performance administration sucks resources from performers. Copious data create a complex quagmire of meaningless mathematics. Managers manage by numerical unthought (Henman 2013). Performers are placed into distorted positions of performance acrobatics to make the numbers dance. The governance by performance measurement becomes iatrogenic.

Learning performance lessons

But, it need not be this way. Instead of dancing to numbers, performance systems, managers, public service actors and public service users need to dance the delicate balance beam of performance measurement contradictions and tensions. This requires insight and nimbleness of mind. Performance measurement can then be powerful and transformative in a positive way, and this is the reason for my own paradox; I both like and dislike performance measurement!; meaning that they make visible new spaces and processes for insight and governance, but they do so problematically and with limited veracity particularly when taken as objective statements of fact about the world that they purport to measure, and used in an algebraic manner that displaces critical, reflective thought about what this new data can and cannot tell us about a phenomenon.

To conclude, successful performance governance requires critical reflection and a willingness to both respect and disrespect performance numbers, to learn from a detailed understanding of performance processes (not just what the numbers denote), consider the dynamics of performance governance retold in the 2011 movie *Moneyball*, staring Brad Pitt as Billy Beane, the general manager of the Oakland Athletics baseball team. Peter Brand (played by Jonah Hill) convinces Billy that algorithms and mathematics is able to destabilise and 'cut through' biases and preconceptions about what makes a player valuable in a league team: 'It's about getting things down to one number'. This performance measurement approach meets very strong resistance from the club. The idea that a quality baseball team can be codified is vilified:

> You don't put a team together with a computer Billie ... baseball isn't just numbers. If there was a science ... Then they would do it. But they can't because they don't know what we know. They don't have our experience and our intuition. Ok. ... There are intangibles that only baseball people understand. (Grady Fuson)

Billy and Peter eventually win the argument given the club's poor finances to purchase players using traditional valuations, and assembles a team using numbers that reflect the combination of players as a dynamic combination, not as a collection of individuals. On paper – not as traditional Curriculum Vitae and socially valorised characteristics, but as numbers – the new team look good, but initially they do not perform where it counts, on the field. The naysayers continue:

> ... the Oakland A's were not a fundamentally sound baseball team. I mean they had a flawed concept ... you can't approach baseball from a statistical bean counting point of view. It's won on the field with fundamental plays .... And you don't do that with a bunch of statistical gimmicks.

Billie is forced to critically reflect on the numbers and what makes the players and numbers dance. He recognises the dark matter that makes a team, and in turn builds team spirit, commitment and comradery. As a consequence, the team then creates a new record in the American league by winning 20 consecutive games.

Numbers count, but they do not count without a qualitative understanding that enables them to dance, and the desired performance to perform. This is the challenge of performance measurement and performance governance.

Note

1. The purpose here is similar to that of Hood (2012) who argues that performance is enhanced consequent to the form of performance governance (targets, rankings or intelligence) and the culture in which performance governance takes place (hierarchist, individualist, egalitarian and fatalism). There are some important synergies and departures in what we each cover.

Acknowledgements

The feedback from reviewers and from workshop participants who heard an earlier presentation of this paper is gratefully acknowledged.

Disclosure statement

No potential conflict of interest was reported by the author.

Funding information

This paper is based on research conducted with the support of an Australian Research Council Discovery Project [grant number DP110100803].

References

Alonso, William, and Paul Starr, eds. 1989. *The Politics of Numbers*. New York: Russell Sage Foundation.
Amrein, Audrey L., and David C. Berliner. 2002. "High-stakes Testing & Student Learning." *Education Policy Analysis Archives* 10 (18): 1–72.
Ball, Stephen J. 2003. "The Teacher's Soul and the Terrors of Performativity." *Journal of Education Policy* 18 (2): 215–228.
Baudrillard, Jean. 1983. "Simulations" Translated by Paul Foss, Paul Patton, and Philip Beitchman. New York: Semiotext (e).
Bevan, Gwyn, and Christopher Hood. 2006. "What's Measured is What Matters: Targets and Gaming in the English Public Health Care System." *Public Administration* 84 (3): 517–538.
Blastland, Michael, and Andrew W. Dilnot. 2009. *The Numbers Game: The Commonsense Guide to Understanding Numbers in the News, in Politics, and in Life*. Harmondsworth: Penguin.
Bowker, Geoffrey C, and Susan Leigh Star. 2000. *Sorting Things out: Classification and its Consequences*. Cambridge, MA: MIT Press.
Busch, Lawrence. 2011. *Standards: Recipes for Reality*. Cambridge, MA: MIT Press.
Callon, Michel, and Bruno Latour. 1992. "Don't Throw the Baby out with the Bath School! A Reply to Collins and Yearley." In *Science as Practice and Culture*, edited by Andrew Pickering, 343–368. Chicago: University of Chicago Press.
Crotty, James. 2009. "Structural Causes of the Global Financial Crisis: A Critical Assessment of the 'New Financial Architecture'." *Cambridge Journal of Economics* 33 (4): 563–580.
Dean, Mitchell. 2010. *Governmentality: Power and Rule in Modern Society*. London: Sage.
Fard, Hassan Danaee, and Ali Asghar Anvary Rostamy. 2007. "Promoting Public Trust in Public Organizations: Explaining the Role of Public Accountability." *Public Organization Review* 7 (4): 331–344.
Foster, Michele, Paul Henman, Alison Gable, and Michelle Denton. 2016. "Population health performance as primary healthcare governance in Australia: professionals and the politics of performance." *Policy Studies* 37 (6): 521–533.
Gable, Alison, and Bob Lingard. 2016. "NAPLAN data: a new policy assemblage and mode of governance in Australian schooling." *Policy Studies* 37 (6): 567–581.
Gao, Jie. 2009. "Governing by Goals and Numbers: A Case Study in the use of Performance Measurement to Build State Capacity in China." *Public Administration and Development* 29 (1): 21–31.
Grimmelikhuijsen, Stephan G, and Albert J. Meijer. 2014. "The Effects of Transparency on the Perceived Trustworthiness of a Government Organization: Evidence from an Online Experiment." *Journal of Public Administration Research and Theory* 24 (1): 137–157.
Henman, Paul. 2013. "Performance Measurement and the Constitution of Unthought." The Politics and Consequences of Performance Measurement, Melbourne, December 11.
Henman, Paul, and Alison Gable. 2015. ""Schooling" Performance Measurement: The Politics of Governing Teacher Conduct in Australia." *Policy and Society* 34 (1): 63–74.
Hood, Christopher. 2007. "What Happens When Transparency Meets Blame-avoidance." *Public Management Review* 9 (2): 191–210.

Hood, Christopher. 2012. "Public Management by Numbers as a Performance-Enhancing Drug: Two Hypotheses." *Public Administration Review* 72 (s1): S85–S92.

Howard, Cosmo, and Amber Chambers. 2016. "The challenge of quantifying national wellbeing: lessons from the Measures of Australia's Progress initiative." *Policy Studies* 37 (6): 550–566.

Lascoumes, Pierre, and Patrick Le Galès. 2007. "Introduction: Understanding Public Policy Through its Instruments." *Governance: An International Journal of Policy. Administration, and Institutions* 20 (1): 1–21.

Latour, Bruno. 1992. "Where are the Missing Masses? The Sociology of a few Mundane Artifacts." In *Shaping Technology/Building Society*, edited by Wiebe E. Bijker and John Law, 225–258. Cambridge: MIT Press.

Latour, Bruno, and Steve Woolgar. 2013. *Laboratory Life: The Construction of Scientific Facts*. Princeton, NJ: Princeton University Press.

Law, John. 2004. *After Method: Mess in Social Science Research*. London: Routledge.

Law, John, Evelyn Ruppert, and Mike Savage. 2011. "The Double Social Life of Methods." Centre for Research on Socio-Cultural Change.

Le Galès, Patrick. 2011. "Policy Instruments and Governance." In *The Sage Handbook of Governance*, edited by Mark Bevir, 142–160. London: Sage.

Le Galès, Patrick. 2016. "Performance measurement as a policy instrument." *Policy Studies* 37 (6): 508–523.

Le Grand, Julian. 1997. "Knights, Knaves or Pawns? Human Behaviour and Social Policy." *Journal of social policy* 26 (2): 149–169.

Miller, Peter, and Nikolas Rose. 2008. *Governing the Present*. Cambridge: Polity.

Power, Michael. 1997. *The Audit Society*. Oxford: Oxford University Press.

Thompson, Edward P. 1967. "Time, Work-discipline, and Industrial Capitalism." *Past and present* 38: 56–97.

Tilbury, Clare. 2016. "Repositioning prevention in child protection using performance indicators." *Policy Studies* 37 (6): 582–595.

Verbeek, Peter Paul. 2010. *What Things do*. University Park: The Pennsylvania State University Press.

Volante, Louis. 2004. "Teaching to the Test: What Every Educator and Policy-maker Should Know." *Canadian Journal of Educational Administration and Policy* 35. September 25, https://www.umanitoba.ca/publications/cjeap/articles/volante.html.

Wastell, David, Sue White, Karen Broadhurst, Susan Peckover, and Andrew Pithouse. 2010. "Children's Services in the Iron Cage of Performance Management: Street-level Bureaucracy and the Spectre of Švejkism." *International Journal of Social Welfare* 19 (3): 310–320.

Willing, Esther. 2016. "Hitting the target without missing the point: New Zealand's immunisation health target for two year olds." *Policy Studies* 37 (6): 534–549.

Winner, Langdon. 1980. "Do Artifacts Have Politics?" *Daedalus* 109 (1): 121–136.

Index

Abbott, A. 72–3
Aboriginal communities 88–9
abuse 86, 88–93, 95
accountability 4, 20, 24–6, 28–33, 37; and child protection 85–6; and immunisation health targets 38–40, 44–5, 47, 50; and school policy assemblages 71–3, 75–8, 80, 82; and techniques/paradoxes 100–1, 107
Accounting, Organization and Society 11
accreditation 26, 28, 32
accuracy 101–2
achievability 103
agreement 102–3
Alastalo, M. 87
armies 12
assemblages 70–84
Assistant Regional Directors (ARDs) 7, 72–3, 75–8, 81–2
audience democracy 6, 15, 26, 31, 33, 71, 103
audit societies 4, 11, 72, 88, 107
Australasia 5
Australia 2, 6–7, 23–36, 53–84, 88–9, 92, 95, 101–2
Australian Bureau of Statistics (ABS) 54, 58–64, 66
Australian Council for Educational Research 72
Australian Curriculum, Assessment and Reporting Authority (ACARA) 72
Australian Medical Association (AMA) 26
Australian Parliamentary Hansard 65
Australian Research Council 75
Austria 13
authenticity 59, 101, 103, 106–7
authoritarianism 13, 18
autonomy 7, 15, 24–5, 28–9, 32, 92, 100, 107

Bauman, Z. 56
benchmarking 1–3, 18–19, 28, 72, 74–7, 81
best practice 15, 86–7
Better Life Index 54
Bevan, G. 103
bias 58, 62, 108
big data 64
Blewett, J. 87
Bligh, A. 72

Bodin, J. 12
Bourdieu, P. 11
Britain 2, 11, 14, 18–19, 87, 89
Bromley, P. 71, 73, 78
bureaucracy 4, 16–18, 20, 28, 32–3, 75, 90

cameral sciences 12–13
capitalism 10, 15, 17–19, 55
carbon emissions 2
case studies 27, 42–7, 55, 71, 73, 75
Cashin, C. 26
centralisation 18
Chambers, A. 6, 53–69, 105
champions 7, 44, 46–7
Chi, Y.-L. 26
child protection 2, 7, 85–98, 101, 104–5
China 4
Christianity 55
citizenship 63
civil servants 13
civil society 13, 53, 74
clarity 101–2
coercion 16, 18, 26, 89, 91, 93–4, 96
Collateral Debt Obligations 107
colonialism 59
command and control 4, 24, 71
communism 55
community sector 93, 96
competition 10–11, 15–16, 19, 30, 45–6, 50, 73, 103
complex societies 14–15, 20
construct validity 6, 101
consumer choice 6, 19
contextual issues 106–7
contracts 1, 3, 19, 25, 27, 32, 39, 44, 47, 73, 92–3
corporatisation 30
criminal justice system 89–90
Croatia 66
Crouch, C. 17
curriculum development 2, 70, 72–3
customer service 3

Dardot, P. 19
dashboard approach 54, 58–60, 62–3, 66

INDEX

data traces 106–7
databases 27, 39, 48, 71, 75
Davidson, K. 61
decoupling 56, 64, 71, 73–5, 78–80, 82
Delamare, N. 13
democracy 4, 6, 10, 13, 15; and national well-being 55, 57, 61; and primary healthcare governance 26, 31, 33; and school policy assemblages 71; and techniques/paradoxes 103
Denmark 91
Denton, M. 23–36
Desrosières, A. 11, 18
deviance 86
digitisation 4
discipline 13, 18, 20, 32
District Health Boards (DHBs) 39–50
diversion 89–90, 92–6
Divisions of General Practice 24–6, 31–2
Dowsley, F. 64
dysfunctional consequences 37–8, 44, 48, 50

Ecological Footprint 58
ecology 56
Edgefield State School (ESS) 75, 79–82
educational attainment 87, 90
efficiency 3–4, 12, 14, 16, 26, 28, 38, 47, 50, 65, 85
Eisenhower, D. 56
élites 14, 18, 20
England 32, 38, 48, 73, 87–8
Enlightenment 12, 55
environment 14–16, 18–19, 54, 56–8, 61, 64
Environmental Sustainability Index 58
episteme 99–100
Escher, M.C. 100, 104
Espeland, W.N. 16
étatisation 11
ethics 27, 48, 100
ethnicity 41, 50
Europe 11, 13, 15–17, 55, 86
European Union (EU) 14
exchequers 12
exclusion 57, 66, 95

family support 86, 89–96
feedback 28, 31, 78
financial crisis 107
Finland 91
Fordism 4
Foster, M. 6–7, 23–36, 101–2
Foucault, M. 11–13, 17, 19
France 19, 54
fraud 2, 102, 106
Freedom House 66
Freedom Index 66
Freidson, E. 32
funding 24–5, 29, 39–40, 43–9, 72–3, 87–8, 91, 93–4
further research 62, 66

Gable, A. 6–7, 23–36, 70–84, 105
gaming 2, 38, 48, 50, 87, 101–3, 107
gatekeepers 23
general medical practitioners (GPs) 7, 23–33, 102
Genuine Progress Indicator (GPI) 54, 61
Genuine Savings 57
German Environmental Economic Accounting 58
Germany 13, 58
Gilbert, N. 86
Gillard, J. 2
Global Education Reform Movement 73
globalisation 10, 17–19
Goa, J. 4
good practice 87, 91
governance 1–7, 11, 13, 16–17, 54; and child protection 92–3; and national well-being 61, 63; new governance 14; and policy assemblages 70–84; and primary healthcare 23–36; and techniques/paradoxes 99, 101–3, 108–9
governmentality 17–20, 108
GPI 57
Great Teachers = Great Results 73
Green GDP 57
gross domestic product (GDP) 2, 6, 53–4, 57–8, 61, 64–6
Gross National Happiness 58
Gupta, A. 87

Hall, J. 65
Halpern, C. 11
Happy Planet Index (HPI) 54, 58
health 6–7, 13–16, 19, 56–7, 61; and child protection 90–4; *Health Community Reports* 26, 30; and immunisation rates 37–52; and national well-being 64; and primary healthcare governance 2, 23–36; and school policy assemblages 75; and techniques/paradoxes 101–4
hegemony 18, 53–4, 64–5
Henman, P. 1–10, 23–36, 99–111
Hill, J. 108
Hood, C. 10, 103
hospitals 26, 38–9, 88
Howard, C. 6, 53–69, 105
Howe, D. 94
Human Development Index (HDI) 54, 58, 65–6
human resources 3

iatrogenesis 108
identity 32, 79
ideology 13, 18–19
Immunisation Advisory Centre 43
Immunisation Coordinators 43
immunisation rates 7, 37–52, 101–3
improvement 7, 16, 24–6, 30, 32; and child protection 87–90, 92–5; and immunisation health targets 37–8, 41–50; and national well-being 54–5, 61; and school policy

INDEX

assemblages 71–3, 75–82; and techniques/paradoxes 101–3, 105, 107
incentives 4, 6, 15–16, 24–6, 29, 31, 45, 102–3, 107
Independent Public Schools 73
Index of Socio-Educational Advantage (ICSEA) 72, 75, 77, 102
Index of Sustainable Economic Welfare 57
Indigenous communities 39, 88–9, 91–2
individualism 3, 13, 24, 56, 95, 103
inequities 11, 18, 39, 41–3, 50, 82, 86, 91–2, 96
information asymmetry 4
information technology 93, 99
innovation 14–16, 56
institutionalisation 14, 18
instrumentation 14–16, 18–20
interdisciplinarity 26
interventionism 15–16, 25, 56, 72, 74, 89–91, 93–4, 96

Jessop, B. 10
journals 11
judiciaries 12

key performance indicators (KPIs) 1–2, 7, 26
Keynes, J.M. 19, 55–7, 64

large firms 10, 18, 30
Lascoumes, P. 5–6, 11, 25–6, 33, 71, 99
Laval, C. 19
Lawn, M. 73, 76
Le Galès, P. 2, 5–6, 10–22, 25–6, 33, 71, 99, 103
Le Grand, J. 103
leadership 38–9, 44, 73, 77–82
league tables 6, 45–6, 50, 107
Leeder, S. 27
legislation 1, 15–16, 86, 88, 91, 93
Levy, J. 18
Lewis, J. 32
liberalism 12, 55
Lingard, B. 6–7, 70–84, 105

McDonald, R. 32
macroeconomics 55–7
Majoribanks, T. 32
Malta 66
maltreatment 90, 92, 94, 96
management sciences 15
managerialism 3, 11, 19–20, 77–8, 81, 86, 100
Māori communities 39, 41–3
marketisation 3–4
Marxism 10, 18, 55
Masters, G. 72
Measures of Australia's Progress (MAP) 53–69
mechanisms 103
media 45, 64, 72–3, 79, 86
Medicare 23, 27
Medicare Locals (MLs) 24–32, 102
Melbourne Declaration of Goals for Australia's Schools 71

mentoring 78
Mertens, D. 18
meta-instruments 24, 29
Miller, P. 17
mixed economies 3
modernity 11, 54–6, 58, 64–6
monarchies 12
monitoring 4, 24, 27–8, 38, 40, 43–5, 48–50, 57, 80, 85–7, 92–3
Munro, E. 87
My School 70–2, 77

Napoleon, Emperor 13
National Accounting Matrix Environmental Accounts 58
National Assessment Program - Literacy and Numeracy (NAPLAN) 70–84, 101
National Health Service (NHS) 38, 48
National Immunisation Register (NIR) 39, 41, 45, 50
National Immunisation Schedule 39
National Partnerships 72
neglect 86, 88–93, 95
neo-institutionalism 18
neo-liberalism 4, 10–11, 18–20, 53, 56, 94, 100
neo-Marxism 10, 18
Netherlands 89
networks 3–4, 14, 17, 19, 24, 26, 43, 47–8
New Deal 57
New Labour 18
New Public Management (NPM) 3–4, 18, 20
New Zealand 7, 37–52, 101–2
Newman, C. 72–3
Nisbett, R. 55
nongovernment sector 75, 88, 92–3, 96
North Korea 66
NVIVO 27, 75

OECD 3, 5, 54
OneSchool 76
ontology 6, 99–100
organisational structures 3, 7, 17, 24, 27–30; and immunisation health targets 37–8, 47–8; and primary healthcare governance 32–3; and school policy assemblages 73–6, 78, 81; and techniques/paradoxes 101, 103, 106
outcomes 1, 3–5, 7, 18, 20, 23–6; and child protection 86–7, 89–90, 95; and immunisation health targets 41, 48; and national well-being 55–6; and primary healthcare governance 31–2; and school policy assemblages 70–2, 74–81; and techniques/paradoxes 101–2, 105–6

Palaszczuk, A. 73
Parton, N. 93
pedagogy 70, 81
performance indicators 3, 6, 11, 15–16, 19–20; and child protection 85–98; key performance indicators 1–2, 7, 26; Performance State 1–4, 10–11; and school policy assemblages 71, 76

INDEX

performance measurement (PM) 1–9, 24–5, 27–30, 37, 40; and child protection 85–8; and health targets 38, 42–6, 50; and national well-being 53, 57–8, 62–4, 66; and paradoxes 99, 103–11; performance chains 102; performance regimes 1; Performance State 1–4, 10–11; as policy instrument 10–22; and primary healthcare governance 23–36; as rationalisation 17–18; and school policy assemblages 71–3, 75–9; and techniques 99–111
philosophy 6, 12
Pitt, B. 108
placement stability 87–91, 95–6
Poland 66
Polanyi, K. 18
police 12–13, 88, 93
policy instruments 2, 5–7, 10–22, 25–6, 32–3; and child protection 85–6, 95–6; definitions 15; and immunisation health targets 38; meta-instruments 24, 29; policy enactment 74; policy objectives 105–6; policy-making 1–9, 14–17, 70–84; and school policy assemblages 71, 73–4, 76; and techniques/paradoxes 99–100; and technologies of government 11–13, 18
political economy 17–18
political science 10
Pollitt, C. 3
population health performance 23–36
Portugal 66
Poso, T. 87
poverty 2, 80, 92, 94
Powell, W. 71, 73, 78
Power, M. 11, 33, 96
power relations 12, 14, 76
Practice Incentive Program (PIP) 26
prevention programmes 92, 94
Primary Health Networks (PHNs) 24, 27, 33
Primary Health Organisations (PHOs) 39, 43, 46–7, 50
primary healthcare governance 2, 23–36
Primary HealthCare Organisations (PHCOs) 24–7, 29–33
principal-agent problem 4
principals 4, 71–82
privacy 48, 93
private sector 10, 16, 28, 30–1, 33, 39, 103
privatisation 18
proceduralisation 12, 19–20, 86–7, 90
professional practices 7, 23–36
professionalism 31–2, 78, 87, 100
Programme for International Student Assessment (PISA) 2
progress 40, 53–64, 66, 81, 89, 100
Prussia 12–13
Public Health Physicians 43
public reporting 26–8, 30–3, 45–6, 53, 72, 76
public sector 2, 4–5, 10, 16, 33, 75, 100, 107
public services 1–9
publication 103, 106

quantification 3, 5, 10–11, 17–20, 53–69, 87, 95
Queensland Child Protection Commission of Inquiry (QCPCI) 88, 95
Queensland Department of Education 71–2, 76, 79

rankings 10, 16, 18–20, 45–6, 50, 53, 103, 107
rationalisation 10–11, 13, 17–20, 74, 81
rationalism 4, 12–14, 18, 53, 85–6, 102, 108
reflective practice 7, 20, 99–111
risk society 87
Rose, N. 17
royal prerogative 12
Rudd, K. 70
Russia 13

Sahlberg, S. 73
Sauder, M. 16
Saudi Arabia 66
School Performance Assessment Framework 82
School Performance Profile 75
schools 2, 6–7, 12, 27, 70–84, 88, 95, 101–2, 105
Schumpeter, J. 10
Scott, A. 16
Slovakia 66
social construction 58, 96
social media 59
social sciences 12, 96, 100, 104–5
social work 87, 91, 95
socialisation 32
socio-political dimensions 1–9
sociology 11, 13, 15, 17–18, 56
solipsism 105
sovereignty 12
stagflation 56
stakeholders 11, 15, 24–5, 27, 59–60, 74, 85–6
standardisation 18, 20, 24–6, 28, 32, 66, 74, 80, 87, 95
state 91, 93, 96, 100, 102; and child protection 85–98; and immunisation health targets 37–52; and national well-being 53–69; and performance measurement 1–9; and policy instruments 10–22; and primary healthcare governance 23–36; and rationalisation 17–18; reshaping of 14–17; and school policy assemblages 70–84; and statisation 12–13; and techniques/paradoxes 99–111; welfare state 14, 23
statistics 11, 18–19, 30, 54, 59–60, 62, 64–6, 71–2, 77, 102, 109
Stiglitz Commission 54, 59
stigmatisation 91, 102
Streeck, W. 17–18
Sturmberg, J. 33
surveillance 18
Syria 66

targets/target-setting 2–3, 37–52, 71–3, 75–7, 79–81, 87, 92, 94–5

INDEX

Teaching and Learning Audit 72
techne 100–3
technical procedures 2, 5–7, 12, 15, 65, 85–7, 92, 95, 99–103, 106
technologies of government 11–13, 18, 100–3
Thatcher, M. 18–19
Tilbury, C. 6–7, 85–98, 101, 105
Torres Strait Islander communities 88–9
transparency 4, 26, 29, 31, 71, 101
Trends in Maths and Science Study 72
Trewin, D. 65
trust 16, 20, 28–9, 31, 33; and child protection 87, 94; and national well-being 55, 57, 61, 65; and school policy assemblages 79; and techniques/paradoxes 101, 107–8
Turquet de Mayenne, L. 12

Union of Soviet Socialist Republics (USSR) 19
United States (US) 11, 17–18
utopias 12

Valentine, K. 95
Ventura, M. 107
Von Justi, J. 13

Weber, M. 10–12, 16–17
welfare state 14, 23
well-being 2, 6, 12, 53–69, 87, 90–1, 95, 101–2, 104–5
Willing, E. 6–7, 37–52, 101–3
Wilson, L. 61
Woodlands State School (WSS) 75, 78–82
World War II (WWII) 57